Nellie Sonet

L-W
BOOK SALES

Collector's Digest
Price Guide to
Carnival Chalkware,
Giveaways and Games

1995 Values

Copyright 1995

Published by
L-W Book Sales
P.O. Box 69
Gas City, IN 46933

ISBN#: 0-89538-036-6

Published by: L-W Book Sales
P.O. Box 69
Gas City, IN 46933

Please write for our free catalog.

Attention Collectors . . . . if you would like to contribute photographs or information of your collection (possibly for profit), please call L-W Books (toll free) at 1-800-777-6450 Tuesday thru Friday, 9am to 3pm.

TABLE OF CONTENTS

PRICING NOTE

When trying to determine the price of the items shown, you should remember the following:

1, Scarcity of the item.
2. Original cost of the item.
3. Whether it is a desirable decorating piece.
4. The condition will have much to do with the price. All prices in the price guide are for pieces in excellent condition.

Below is a chart to help you determine the condition of an item.

1. Mint – brand new, found in original shipping box or paper, never used.
2. Excellent – signs of aging, no wear, chips, or cracks etc.
3. Good – aging, some wear, no chips or cracks.
4. Fair – aging, much wear, small chips, no cracks.
5. Poor – (Not collectible).

INTRODUCTION

Shortly after the final days of World War I, most of our American boys returned home from the front, eager to continue their lives at home with family and friends. The economy was prospering with the war effort complete and the Industrial Revolution in full swing. The American public required entertainment and relaxation to fulfill their now-available leisure time, and the more common forms of entertainment included the movies, circuses, amusement parks, and when it was in town, the *Carnival.*

Promoters presented carnivals and circuses to provide a variety of live entertainment, fun-filled family games, and other diversions to place a smile on a weary face. Smaller shows ranged from three to four rides with a dozen game joints to enormous shows setting up at state fairs.

Game operators by the hundreds would travel throughout the country, as an established unit of a carnival caravan or perhaps merely a loner setting up shop in another remote rural town, week after week. During business hours (late afternoon or evening for their line of work) they would then lure courageous or brawny men to attempt to win a prize for their blushing bride-to-be or to take home for their daughters. These prizes were won in basketball shoots, milk bottle throws, dart games, hoop tosses, duck ponds, and many other clever games designed to lighten the pocketbook. As these contests were often rigged in the operator's favor, usually you would only win if he so desired.

Many older gentlemen today recall going to the carnival with a dollar or two with dreams of winning pocketfuls of penny prizes and returning home with no money.

Some of the games provided were outright gambling schemes. Most of the operators were crooked and worked with an accomplice or shill to make it appear simple to win. Many players would be enticed into the game and end up losing the week's paycheck. The three shell game with a pea, three card monte, and other sleight of hand games were most often used.

Many of the prizes and equipment are now collectibles and can be found at many shows and flea markets.

The book originally entitled *Midway Mania* was the original book on the subject. The challenge of winning these chalkware prizes and difficult dexterity sports or guessing games no longer exists, yet the challenge of finding them remains.

Animal Statues

Blue Birds, 8" x 8"
(one painted red, the other blue).

WWII Dog, 4" x 5".   Bird Ashtray, 5" x 8".

Animal Statues

Owl, 5" x 11".   Ferdinand the Bull, 5" x 9".

(Left to Right)
Collie Dog, 9" x 11"   Dog with ball, 8" x 9"   Pekinese, 6" x 9"

Animal Statues

Imitation Staffordshire Dog, 8" x 11".

Parrot, 5" x 13"

Animal Statues

White Cat, 6" x 17"
Yellow Cat with Hat, 4" x 9".

Animal Statues

Pig, 5" x 12".   Dog with Hat, 5" x 10"

Elephant Statues
Left: 9" x 10 ½"   Right: 9" x 12"

Animal Statues

Two King Kong statues, 8" x 15" each.

Animal Statues

Lion, 10" x 12".

Tiger, 8" x 16".

Animal Statues/Clown

Circus Elephant, 6" x 14".   Clown, 6" x 12 1/2"

Ship, 9" x 10"   Lighthouse, 8" x 11"

Statues

Left: Snow White, 6" x 15".

Right: Cowboy, 5" x 11".

Pinocchio Statues

Left: 5" x 14"
Right: 6" x 15"

Girl/Doll Statues etc.

(Left to Right)
Hula Girl with cloth skirt, 4" x 15"
Hula Girl with tinsel trim, 7" x 17"
Hula Girl with no skirt, 4" x 16".

Girl/Doll Statues etc.

Hula Girl, 4" x 9 1/2",
signed: Made by Indianapolis
Statuary Co..

1920's Betty Boop, 4" x 13'.
Seated Flapper, 3" x 7"

Left to Right:

Little Egypt, 7" x 13",
(late teens), rare.

1920's Kewpie Lamp,
4" x 13".

Girl/Doll Statues etc.

Kewpie Doll Statues
Left to Right: 7" x 12½" • 4" x 8" • 7" x 12½"

Left to Right
Kewpie Doll with crepe paper skirt, 3" x 9"
Kewpie Doll with arms out, 9" x 13"
Kewpie Doll seated, 3" x 8"

Girl/Doll Statues etc.

Bag Pipe Girls, 6" x 15 1/2"

Girl/Doll Statues etc.

Drum Majorettes, 5" x 16"

Girl/Doll Statues etc.

Sweater Girls, 6" x 15".

Girl/Clown Statues

Mary Had A Little Lamb, 7" x 16".
Clown, 6" x 12 1/2"

Military Statues

Eagle (Victory), 8" x 13".
General MacArthur, 7" x 9"

George Washington
Two Small Ones – 6" x 7 1/2"
Large – 9" x 11"

Military Statues

1941 Soldier Statue, 5" x 15"
1942 Sailor Statue, 5" x 15"

Military/Uncle Sam Statues

Sailor Boy, 4" x 13"   Sailor Girl, 5" x 14".

Uncle Sam Statues: Left – 7" x 14"   Right – 4" x 16"

Military Statues

WWII Civil Defense Man, 5" x 14"
WWII Cannon with Sailor, 7" x 13"

Military/Cowboys/Indians etc.

Indian, 3" x 8"   Sailor, 3" x 8"

Indian on Horse, 9" x 10", signed St. Louis Art Toy Co.
Cowboy on Horse, 9" x 10 1/2"

Novelties

Left: Feather Girl on Bamboo Cane   Right: Figural Canes

Photographers prop, elephant is 7'6" tall x 3' wide.

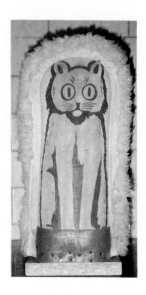

Cloth Cat, 14" high.

Carnival Games

Ornate Roulette Wheel, 24" diameter.

Roulette Wheel, 10" diameter.

Astrological Reading Machine, approximately 1' x 2' x 6'.

Huey Duck, 4" x 7"
Pig 4" x 7"

Cat, 4" x 7"
Scottie, 3" x 7"

Chipmunk, 3" x 5"
Bunny, 3" x 7"

Comic Dog, 4" x 7"
Dog with Pipe, 4" x 6"

Charlie McCarthy, 3" x 7"
Charlie McCarthy, 5" x 17"

Indian, 4" x 16"
Indian Bust, 7" x 13"

Long Ranger, 6" x 15"
Superman, 6" x 16" (rare)

Rooster, 8" x 13"

Ducks, 5" x 14"

1932 Midland Doll Co. Catalog Page

Snug Pup
6" high, very beautifully painted.

Queenee
6" high.

Elephant
comes in different sizes,
4 1/2" high, 9 1/2" high, and 12" high.

Elephant
with blanket and head dress, metallic
tinsel trimming, came in different sizes,
9 1/2" high, and 12" high.

1932 Midland Doll Co. Catalog Page

Boston Bull Dog
with glass eyes, comes in different
sizes, 7" high and 10" high.

Police Dog

Rin Tin Tin
12" high, tinsel trimmed.

Pekinese Dog
8 1/2" high, with glass eyes.

1932 Midland Doll Co. Catalog Page

Oriental Ball Girl
19" high, natural color, best lacquer
finish with metallic tinsel cap and belt.

Bathing Doll
enamel finish, beautifully painted,
imported metallic tinsel bathing suit.

Beach Belle
natural color, enamel finish, metallic
tinsel bathing suit in assorted colors.

Frenchy
17" high, very fancy,
specially painted in attractive colors.

1932 Midland Doll Co. Catalog Page

Pussy Cat
6" high.

Lilly Doll
10 ½" high, with metallic tinsel bathing
suit in assorted colors. The shell is
painted to match the doll.

Tootle
11" high, with long curly hair,
and 30" of tinsel hoop dress.

1936 Pacini Novelty Statuary Co. Catalog Page

Colt and Circus Horse
8 1/2" high, with bright silver tinsel.

Junior Cowboy on Horse
11 1/2" high, assorted colors trimmed
in silver tinsel.

Broncho Buster
15" high, with removable hat.

The Gay Buckaroo
16" high, Broncho Buster's Big Brother,
western colors, with removable hat.

LEVIN BROS., TERRE HAUTE, IND.

"De Luxe" Plaster Novelty Assortments

10% will be added to orders for less than original cartons

14c Each   Novelty Assortment   **14c** Each

N9761—Plaster Novelty Assortment. (Mfrs 1) A new and original assortment in a price range that will fill a most popular demand. The characters are of modernistic design, with high lustre finishes and of generous size. Packed 36 assorted pieces in carton, weight 50 lbs.

Per carton (36 pieces) **$5.04**

Special Plaster Assortment

25c Each

25c Each

N9760—Special Plaster Assortment (Mfrs 34) Six of the most popular numbers are included in this assortment. The number not shown is N9764 baby elephant. These numbers have been carefully chosen to fill the most particular demands. Adaptable for Corn Games, Scale, Bowling Alleys, Ball Games, etc. You will agree that this is the biggest value ever offered in composition goods. Packed 24 assorted pieces in carton, weight 50 lbs.

Per carton (24 pieces) **$6.00**

N9760H—Horses only as illustrated ½ doz in carton **$3.00**

1935 Catalog Page

"De Luxe" Quality Plaster Dolls and Elephants
Improved Design—Construction—Packing

NOTE: 50 per cent deposit must accompany C. O. D. orders, otherwise shipment will not be made. We are not responsible for breakage in transit.

Each 25c

DeLuxe Sheba Doll. (Mfrs. 31.) High lustre finish in beautiful colors with large plumes to match, height of doll 23 in., 24 in carton; (wt. 48 lbs.)

N9848—With Turkey Feather Plumes. Each $0.25
Carton (24 pcs.) 6.00

N9848X — With Ostrich Feather Plumes. Each........... .30
Carton (24 pcs.) .. 7.20

Each 22c

N9845—Vamp Doll. (Mfrs. 12.) Height 13 in., painted hair, dressed in assorted color floral crepe dresses. Shipped completely dressed, 24 in carton, assorted finishes, dolls and dresses (weight 48 lbs.)
Per carton ... $5.28

Each 24c

N9847—Ruby Doll. (Mfrs 19.) Height 12 in.; painted bobbed hair, large colored crepe oval dress tinsel trimmed, very easy to match. Packed 24 in carton (weight 36 lbs.)
Per carton $5.76

● **10%** will be added to orders for less than original cartons. ●

Each 20c

Each 45c

N9766—Jumbo Elephant. (Mfrs 10.) Height 13 in. Decorated in a wide variety of bright colors, nicely blended, blanket and decorations trimmed with wide borders of metallic tinsel, 18 assorted in barrel (weight 100 lbs.)
Per barrel $8.10

N9851—Daisy Doll. (Mfrs 20.) Natural finish with hand painted sweetheart bob Assorted colored one piece hat and dress decorated with heavy tinsel. High lustre finish doll with hand painted eyes; height 14½ in., 24 assorted in carton, (weight 36 lbs.)
Per carton $4.80

Each 25c

N9764—Baby Elephant. (Mfrs 7.) An exact duplicate in color and design of the Jumbo Elephant on opposite side of page Height 10 in.; lightweight, packed 24 assorted in carton (weight 50 lbs.)
Per carton $6.00

1936 Pacini Novelty Statuary Co. Catalog Page

Scotty
10" high, finished in natural colors.

My Pal
9" high, rhinestone eyes,
trimmed with shiny tinsel.

Police Dog Ashtrays
6" high, finished in
assorted natural colors.

Scotty Dog Ashtray
6" high, natural colors.

1936 Pacini Novelty Statuary Co. Catalog Page

Dancing Doll
14" high, assorted colors,
trimmed with tinsel.

Fan Dancer
15" high, made of composition, all
painted features, tinsel slippers.

Miss Katy of the Nineties
14" high, lady of the past century,
trimmed with silver tinsel.

Rebecca Lamp
14 1/2" high, a radio and table lamp,
finished in bronzes.

1936 Pacini Novelty Statuary Co. Catalog Page

Popeye
13 1/2" high, finished in natural
contrasting colors, with real pipe.

Wimpy
13" high, hamburger champ,
finished in natural colors.

Jumbo and Dolly
10 1/2" high, circus elephant
and performer.

Elephant of India
9 1/2" high, trimmed in silver tinsel.

1940 Catalog Page

COMPOSITION PLASTER FIGURES
ARTISTICALLY DECORATED

No. 672 — Sport Girl. Appealing new design made of plaster composition and painted in beautiful assorted bright color combinations with sparkling tinsel decorations. Height, 15¼ inches. Packed 12 in a carton (29 lbs.) (No less sold.)

Each .... 13½¢

No. 681 — Circus Horse with Plume. Made of plaster composition and painted in attractive colors with sparkling tinsel decorations. Height, 11⅛ inches; length, 9¼ inches. Packed 12 in a carton (30 lbs.) (No less sold.)

Each .... 13½¢

No. 655—Ranger. Realistic likeness of a famous cartoon character. Made of plaster composition in assorted color combinations with sparkling tinsel decorations. Height, 11⅛ inches. Packed 12 assorted colors in shipping carton (28 lbs.) (No less sold.)

Each .... 13½¢

No. 655—Indian on Horse. Made of plaster composition in assorted brightly colored finishes. The Chief's head-dress as well as the base are decorated with sparkling tinsel. Height, 10¼ inches. Packed 12 in a carton (23 lbs.). (No less sold.)

Each .... 13½¢

No. 652—Novelty Dutch Windmill. An unusually beautiful new design made of plaster composition and realistically painted in bright color combinations with sparkling tinsel decorations. An exceptionally appealing value. Height, 10 inches; width, 6¼ inches. Packed 12 in a shipping carton (22 lbs.) (No less sold.)

Each .... 13½¢

No. 665—Ranger on Horse. Made of plaster composition and painted in bright colors with sparkling tinsel decorations. Height, 10¾ inches; length, 9 inches. Packed 12 in a carton (25 lbs.) (No less sold.)

Each .... 13½¢

No. 683—Jumbo Comical Bull. Ties up with the unsurpassed popularity of comical bulls. New Jumbo design—fatter and funnier than anything we've ever offered. Plaster composition in assorted bright color combinations with sparkling tinsel decorations. Height, 9¾ inches. Packed 6 in a carton (15 lbs.) (No less sold.)

Each .... 17¢

No. 656—"Rex" Police Dog. This is the biggest selling plaster composition novelty on the market. Beautifully molded in the shape of a German Police Dog standing on base. High lustre lacquer finish in assorted colors with sparkling tinsel on collar and base. Height, 10¼ inches. Packed 12 assorted colors in carton (28 lbs.) (No less sold.)

Each .... 13½¢

1940 Catalog Page

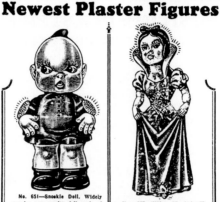

1940 Catalog Page

DECORATED PLASTER NOVELTIES and
ANIMAL ASSORTMENTS

No. 650—Novelty Stage Coach Electric Lamp. Made of plaster composition, attractively finished in harmonizing color effects. Very heavily decorated with sparkling tinsel. Complete with regulation size cord and plug. Length, 19 inches; height, 9½ inches. Packed 6 to the shipping carton (30 lbs.). (No less sold.)
Each..................................55¢

No. 680—Comical Sailorman. A new plaster composition novelty. Painted in bright colors and decorated with sparkling tinsel and is an excellent caricature of a sailor. Height, 12 inches. Packed 12 in a carton (14 lbs.) (No less sold.)
Each..................13½¢

No. 663—Midget Plaster Animal Assortment. An attractive variety of animals such as dogs, cats, etc., realistically made of plaster composition in beautiful high lustre finish assorted color combinations. Average height, 5 inches. Packed 100 assorted in a carton (47 lbs.) (No less sold.)
Each..................5¢

No. 660—Dancing Elephant. A handsome new plaster composition novelty, appealingly painted in assorted natural and bright color combinations with sparkling tinsel decorations. Plenty of flash at an unusually low price. Height, 10½ inches. Packed 12 assorted in a carton (21 lbs.). (No less sold.)
Each..................12½¢

No. 674 — Sitting Scotty Dog. A new and realistically designed plaster composition novelty appealingly painted in assorted solid black, brown and white, and black and white colors with contrasting color painted features and sparkling tinsel decorations. Height, 9½ inches. Packed 12 assorted colors in a carton (21 lbs.). (No less sold.)
Each..................13½¢

No. 669—Sailor Maid. A clever new plaster composition novelty. Has white body with painted features and beautifully colored trimming. Decorated with sparkling tinsel. Height, 12¾ inches. Packed 12 in a shipping carton (18 lbs.) (No less sold.)
Each..................12½¢

No. 658—Broncho Buster with Felt Hat. An excellent plaster composition reproduction of a cowboy painted in attractive colors with sparkling tinsel decorations. Supplied complete with felt cowboy hat having band with inscription, "Ride 'Em Cowboy." Height with hat, 14½ inches. Packed 12 in a carton (27 lbs.) with hats separate (No less sold.)
Each..................20¢

No. 654—Feature Plaster Assortment. An appealing variety consisting of dogs, circus horses, comical bulls, ventriloquist dummies, Washington on horse, etc. Plaster composition in assorted high lustre finish bright color combinations with sparkling tinsel decorations. An exceptionally attractive assortment. Average height, 6 inches. Packed 24 assorted in a carton (17 lbs.) (No less sold.)
Each..................7½¢

45

GELLMAN BROS, MINNEAPOLIS, MINN.

NEW CREATIONS IN PLASTER FIGURES
AND REALISTIC ANIMALS

IMPORTANT NOTICE

We are not responsible for BREAKAGE in transit and ship PLASTER GOODS by EXPRESS, FREIGHT, OR TRUCK ONLY. No PARCEL POST shipments can be made.

No. 657—Comical Puppet. The unsurpassed popularity of this character makes it a winner! Realistically made of plaster composition and painted in bright assorted color combinations with sparkling tinsel trim. Height, 14½ inches. Packed 12 assorted colors in a carton (29 lbs.). (No less sold.)
Each..................15¢

No. 668—Ancient Ship. Made of plaster composition and painted in assorted bright color combinations with sparkling tinsel decorations. Length, 9½ inches; height, 9½ inches. Packed 12 in a shipping carton (28 lbs.). (No less sold.)
Each....................13½¢

No. 682—Comical Cricket. Realistic likeness of a widely popular cartoon character. Handsomely made of plaster composition in assorted bright color combinations with sparkling tinsel decorations. Height, 13½ inches. Packed 12 in a carton (22 lbs.) (No less sold.)
Each.....................15¢

No. 685—Comical Standing Bull. Another winner that ties up with the widespread popularity of comical bulls. Plaster composition in natural appearing brown color with painted features and artificial flower in mouth. Tinsel decorated. Height, 9½ inches. Packed 12 in a carton (24 lbs.). (No less sold.)
Each......................13½¢

No. 659—African Elephant. Made of plaster composition in assorted colors with contrasting colored trappings and sparkling tinsel decorations. A popular new item that sells fast! Length, 13 inches. Packed 12 assorted colors in a shipping carton (25 lbs.). (No less sold.)
Each.....................13½¢

No. 664—Comical Sitting Bull. Widespread popularity of comical bulls makes this a winner. Plaster composition in natural appearing brown color with painted features and artificial flower in mouth. Tinsel decorated. Height, 9½ inches. Packed 12 in a carton (24 lbs.) (No less sold.)
Each......................13½¢

No. 678—Twin Scotty Dogs. Made of plaster composition and painted in natural appearing assorted red and white, and black and white color combinations with tinsel decorations. Height, 10 inches Packed 12 assorted colors in a shipping carton (30 lbs.). (No less sold.)
Each.............. 13½¢

No. 673—Scotty Dog. Designed of plaster composition in red, white and black color combinations with sparkling tinsel decorations. Height, 10¾ inches, length, 9½ inches. Packed 12 in a carton (31 lbs.) (No less sold.)
Each ..... 13½¢

WHOLESALE PREMIUM MERCHANDISE & NOVELTIES

46

EVANS' KUTIE KIDS

The most popular statuette doll ever offered, 15 inches high, made of wood pulp, handsomely finished.

No. 40A400 Without dress..Per doz. **$10.50**

No. 40A402 Fur trimmed dress..Per doz. **14.50**

INDESTRUCTIBLE CHARACTER DOLLS

1034—Miss Columbia   799—Boy Scout   1002—Red Cross Nurse

These dolls are full 30 inches high, made of the best materials obtainable and well dressed. We carry a wide variety of styles in stock at all times, those illustrated being the most popular.

No. 40A1034 Miss Columbia..Per doz. **$15.50**

No. 40A1002 Red Cross Nurse..Per doz. **15.50**

No. 40A799 Boy Scout..Per doz. **15.75**

1920 Catalog Page

Flash Draws The Crowd

A new line of Electric Lamps and Dolls

No. 468
FLASHY VASE LAMP

20" High —Electric —Unbreakable.

Finished in the new stippled bronzes, red, blue, green, orange gold, silver and copper. Shades made of fine texture silk crepe tissue—with fringe trimming.

Complete with socket, plug and 6 ft. cord—ready to light.

In cartons of 30 and 60

Case of 30	$21.50
Case of 60	42.00

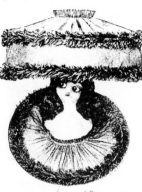

No. 469
DOLL LAMP

20" High --Electric --Unbreakable.

An Ideal Table Lamp—Complete with socket, plug and 6 ft. cord, ready to light. Round shade, assorted colors, trimmed with double rows of fringe and hoop dress--

In cartons of 30 and 60

Case of 30 special at	$21.50
Case of 60 special at	42.00

No. 470-A

THE UNGER TWINS
NON-BREAKABLE

WRAPPED IN BLANKET

Measures 22" High with blanket open as shown. $1.00 per set in cartons of 12 and 36

No. 987   FLASH DOLL

20" High--Unbreakable--The famous Flash Doll--

Air brushed in colors--with Genuine Ostrich Plume Dress. Very attractive.

In cartons of 60

Case of 60 special at $23.50

No. 988   NIFTY DOLL

This catchy doll has a long curly wig, dressed with a Gloria Swanson hat and band. Looks like dollars.

Case of 60 special (15" Doll) $23.50

No. 988-A

Case of 30 Big 25" New Gloria Dolls $29.50

GELLMAN BROS. MINNEAPOLIS, MINN.

Large Size Novelty Celluloid Dolls
Dressed With White and Colored Feathers

No. 2006—"Miss Carole" Celluloid Doll. Strikingly dressed in assorted brightly colored feathers with fancy feather head-dress and appealing painted features. Supplied with jointed arms and has gilt bead necklace and earrings. Assorted silver and gold painted wavy hair effect, with colored metallic paper hats in assorted styles. Height, 10 inches. Packed one dozen assorted in box.

Per dozen.................................**$1.10**
Per gross.................................**$12.50**

No. 2029—"Miss Universe" Celluloid Doll. Strikingly dressed in pure white feathers with white feathers head-dress and fancy assorted color metallic paper high hat. Jointed arm style with alluring painted features, assorted silver and gold painted wavy hair effect decorated with silver tinsel, metallic paper breast decoration, gilt bead earrings, and necklace. Colored celluloid cane attached to hand. Height, 12 inches. One-half dozen assorted in box.

Per dozen.................................**$1.65**
Per gross.................................**$18.50**

No. 2005—"Miss Dolores" Celluloid Doll. Appealing new jointed arm style, dressed in bright assorted color feathers with fancy silver tinseled feather head-dress and beautiful painted features. Has gilt bead earrings and necklace, with assorted silver and gilt painted wavy hair effect and colored celluloid cane attached to hand. Height, 10 inches. Packed one dozen assorted in box.

Per dozen.................................**$1.10**
Per gross.................................**$12.50**

No. 2025—"Miss Patsy" Celluloid Doll. Beautifully dressed in bright assorted color feathers, with fancy feather head-dress and silver tinsel breast and head decorations. Striking painted features with gilt bead necklace, earrings and armlets. Supplied with jointed arms and assorted silver and gilt painted wavy hair effect. Height, 12 inches. Packed one-half dozen assorted in box.

Per dozen.................................**$1.60**
Per gross.................................**$18.00**

No. 2026—"Miss America" Celluloid Doll. Attractive jointed arm style, dressed in bright assorted color feathers with fancy feather head-dress and fancy metallic paper high hats in assorted styles and colors. Has gilt bead earrings, necklace and armlets with beautiful painted features and assorted silver and gilt painted wavy hair effect. Colored celluloid cane attached to hand. Height, 12 inches. Packed one-half dozen assorted in box.

Per dozen.................................**$1.65**
Per gross.................................**$18.50**

No. 2020—"Miss Fifth Avenue" Celluloid Doll. Attractive new style dressed in bright assorted color feathers with fancy feather decorated celluloid head-dress. Jointed arm style with alluring painted features, and silver tinsel breast and head decorations. Supplied with gilt bead necklace and earrings, and assorted silver and gilt painted wavy hair effect. Colored celluloid cane attached to hand. Height, 12 inches. Packed one-half dozen assorted in box.

Per dozen.................................**$1.65**
Per gross.................................**$18.50**

WHOLESALE PREMIUM MERCHANDISE & NOVELTIES

LEVIN BROS., TERRE HAUTE, IND.

NEW GLASS NOVELTIES

Popular Sellers. Used for Favo
Souvenirs, etc.

EXCELLENT FOR PREMIUMS
PRIZE PURPOSES, HOOP-LA GAMES, ETC.

**Very Desirable For
Souvenirs**

N9700. White Cat, made
of crystal glass, 1½ inches
high. Brilliant White Stone
eyes. An excellent orna-
ment or paper weight.
Each in a box.
Per dozen $1.20

N9701. Rooster, made of
glass, 3½ inches high, finished in bright colors, presenting a very natural appearance. Each in a box.
Per dozen $1.20

MEDALLION PAPER WEIGHTS.
N9072. **Paper Weight.** Made of glass, 3¾ inch
in diameter with gilded outline relief figure of Gener
Pershing or Joffre. A very appropriate novelty ar
will be an enormous seller. Each in a box.
Per dozen ....$1.

NOVELTY GLASS WATCH
CHARMS.

N9703   N9704   N9706

N9703. **Rajah Watch Charm.** Made of crystal glass,
Minature white elephant, ¾ inch high, to be worn
on a watch chain, one of the newest novelties of the
season. Per doz........90c. Per gross.......$10.50
N9704. **Midget Dog Watch Charm.** Made of crystal
glass, 9-16 inch high, has brilliant white stone eyes.
To be worn as a watch charm.
Per dozen ....90c. Per gross........$10.50
N9705. **Monkey Watch Charm.** Same as above.
Per dozen ....90c. Per gross..........$10.50
TURKEY PLACE CARD HOLDER.
N9706. **Turkey Place Card Holder,** made of glass,
finished in rich natural colors. A handsome appearing ornament that makes an ideal place card holder
and as a souvenir will be appreciated. Height 2¾
inches. Per dozen $1.20

N9707. **American Eagle,**
made of glass. An elegant
figure of the National bird in
characteristic pose with spread
wings, richly gilded. Height
2¾ inches. Spread 4 inches.
An ornament that is very appropriate at present.

Per dozen $1.20

N9708. **Watermelo
Boy.** An excellen
reproduction, mad
of heavy glass, heigh
2¾ inches. Finishe
in bright colors. Ver
natural appearance.

Per dozen .....$1.2(

Glass and China Novelties

IMITATION DIAMOND EYE-GLASS NOVELTIES

The most artistic line of glass novelties ever produced. Made in satin finish and 3 shades, amber, black and crystal. Fitted with fine cut brilliant whitestone eyes. Each in a box.

N9250. Diamond Eye Elephant, height 2½ inches. Assorted to the dozen, six satin finish crystal, three satin finish amber and three black. Per doz....$1.20

N9251. Diamond Eye Dog, heigh 2¾ inches. Assorted to the dozen, as above. Dozen.........$1.20

N9252. Diamond Eye Cat, height 3 inches. Assorted to the dozen, as above. Dozen.............$1.20

N9253. Diamond Eye Rabbit, height 2¼ inches. Assorted to the dozen, six satin finish crystal, three satin finish amber and three colored. Dozen....$1.20

N9254. Diamond Eye Lion, height 2¼ inches. Assorted to the dozen, as above. Per dozen......$1.20

N9255. Diamond Eye Owl, height 3½ inches. Assorted to the dozen, as above. Per dozen........$1.20

Glass Watches and Revolvers

Resemble the Real Article

YOU CAN SELL THESE AT A LARGE PROFIT

N9256. Glass Watch, an exact duplicate of an 18-size engraved hunting case watch, with metal bow. Perfect in detail, requires close inspection to detect. Each in a box. 2 dozen in a carton. Please order in original cartons.

Per dozen $1.20
Per Gross $13.50

GLASS REVOLVERS

$1.35 Per Dozen

N9257. Glass Revolver, a perfect imitation, made entirely of glass. Ebonized stock, balance in nickel finish, 8 inches long. Can be used as a paper weight, or flash, and in some cases will serve equally as well as the real article on account of its genuine appearance, 2 dozen in a carton. No less sold. Doz...$1.35

CHINA NOVELTY FIGURES

N9258   N9259   N9260

N9258. Jonah and the Whale, figure about 4 inches long, finished in bright colors, features clearly defined in black. 1 dozen in package.
Per dozen ....45c. Per gross $5.25

N9259. China Figures, length about 4 inches, nicely executed body, features clearly defined in bright colors. 1 dozen in package, assorted animals.
Per dozen ....45c. Per gross $5.25

N9260. China Figure, size 3x3½ inches, child riding on an Elephant. Nicely executed and finished in gilt, balance of figure white glazed.
Per dozen ....45c. Per gross $5.25

N9261   N9262   N9263

N9261. Boy and Girl Figures, about 4½ in. high, each on a base, finished in bright colors. 1 dozen assorted in package. Dozen...45c. Gross....$5.25

N9262. Cat and Dog Figures, about 3½ in. high, nicely shaped and proportioned, clearly defined features and finished in colors. 1 dozen assorted in package. Per dozen ......45c. Per gross $5.25

N9263. Spotted Dog Figure, about 2½x4 inches, nicely executed and finished in colors. 1 dozen in package. Per dozen ......45c. Per gross $5.25

N9264   N9265   N9266

N9264. China Chair Figures, assorted cats, dogs and monkeys. Length 2½ inches. Nicely decorated and finished in bright colors. Doz...45c. Gross..$5.25

N9265. China Chair Figures, assorted boys and girls, length about 2½ inches, finished and decorated in appropriate colors. 1 dozen assorted in package. Per dozen ....45c. Per gross $5.25

N9266. Novelty China Dogs, full shaped figures, spiral wire wagging tails, brown glazed china. Per dozen ....45c. Per gross $5.25

Glass Ball Scopes

N9267. Novelty Fish Globe. 1¾ inches diameter, filled with liquid and imitation gold moss with fish inside, mounted on fancy metal base. Excellent souvenir novelty. Each in box, dozen in package.
Per dozen ....60c. Per gross $7.00

N9268. Glass Scopes. High pitch men make big money with this item. 1 gross in box. No less sold. Each in a carton. Per gross....................$4.00

MIDWEST MERCHANDISE CO. KANSAS CITY, MISSOURI 113

NOVELTY CHINA ASH TRAYS

No. Z11350—Novelty Toilet Ash Tray. Consists of a black donkey, pulling a white pot, made of china; highly glazed finish. Length about 5 inches.

Per Dozen. $0.60
Per Gross. $6.00

No. Z11351—Pig Pulling Pot, Novelty Ash Tray. Made of high lustre china, a very comical number. Length about 5 inches.

Per Dozen. $0.75
Per Gross. $8.00

Z11352—Pants Ash Tray. Small size, made of china, bright colors, height about 2½ inches.
Per Dozen **$0.40**
Per Gross **$4.40**

Z11354—Donkey with Saddle Bags Pulling Pot with Wood Lid. This is a very clever ash tray, made in bright finish.

Per Dozen. $0.75
Per Gross. $8.00

No. Z11353 — Novelty China Ash Tray Assortment. Consists of several different kinds of characters pulling pots. Average length about 3½ inches. Packed assorted to box.

Per Dozen. $0.40
Per Gross. $4.40

No. Z11355 — Miniature Ash Tray. Made up for a low price item; assorted sayings. Length about 1½ inches; packed one gross in box. No less sold.
Per Gross. **$1.00**

No. Z11356—Two Pants Ash Tray with colored boy looking through. A nice size ash tray, made up in lustre china. Height about 3½ inches.

Per Dozen $0.75
Per Gross. $8.00

NOVELTY ASH TRAYS—HOTCHA GIRL

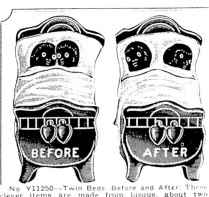

No Y11250—Twin Beds, Before and After. These clever items are made from bisque, about two inches in length, suitably colored. They will make you laugh. Packed one pair in box
Per Dozen............................. **$1.50**

No Y11251—Turn Over Ash Tray. Made of dura the metal gilded, serves also as a paper weight. No one fails to turn them over and then the effect. Packed one dozen in carton
Per Dozen........................... **$1.50**

No Y11252 — Hotcha Girl. A superb figure of a girl in natural flesh color made of a rubber like washable substance, hair eyes, lips and other features are hand painted. Figure mounted on a sturdy steel base which contains a clock spring and when wound she dances like todays busi.....A big hit at the world's fair under a simple quick....

Each **$ 1.00**
Doz **$11.50**

No Y11253 — Novelty Cigarette Extinguisher Ash Tray. Featuring a standing dog with a raised leg and made of bisque. Dog has a small rubber ball fixed to it. As it squeezed the dog performs. A very clever novelty item.
Per Dozen **$1.00**

No Y11254 — Metal Ash Tray. Has tray and bull attached which may be filled with water to be sprayed out by squeezing bull....

Each....................... **$0.25**
Per Dozen............... **$2.50**

NOVELTY SQUIRT ASH TRAYS

No Y11255 — Novelty Extinguisher Ash Tray. Made of glazed marble effect china in attractive shape with figure of monkey seated at the center of ash tray. One hand holds a rubber tube and bulb which can fill the monkey. A light pressure of the bulb squirts the ash.....

Per Dozen **$2.00**

LEVIN BROS., TERRE HAUTE, IND.

Air Guns for Shooting Corks and Concessionaires' Supplies

Daisy Air Rifles for Shooting Corks

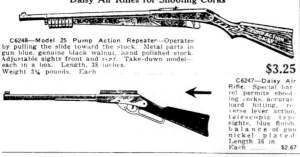

C6248—Model 25 Pump Action Repeater—Operates by pulling the slide toward the stock. Metal parts in gun blue, genuine black walnut, hand polished stock. Adjustable sights front and rear. Take-down model—each in a box. Length, 38 inches. Weight 3¼ pounds. Each

$3.25

C6247—Daisy Air Rifle. Special barrel permits shooting corks, accurate hard hitting, reverse lever action, telescopic type sights, blue finish, balance of gun nickel plated. Length 36 in. Each $2.67

Double Tags for Dart Galleries

N9305. Double Tag—1 in. diameter; two tags riveted together with an eyelet. Put up 1000 in a box, no less sold.
Per 100 .... 50c
Per 1,000 .... $4.50

Corks

C6251—Corks. To be used in the Daisy Air Rifles for cigarette galleries. Put up 500 in a cloth sack.
Per bag............................. 90c

Darts for Air Rifles

C6249—Air Rifle Darts. (Mfrs. 17-100). Can be used with Daisy and King Air Rifles. 1 doz. in envelope.
Doz..........15c   Gro.....$1.75

Hoop La Rings

N9385—Select polished maple, ⅜ inch wide, lathe turned and rounded edges, perfectly true in circle. Put up one dozen pair of a size in a package—no less sold. Furnished in 3, 4, 5, 6 and 7 inch diameter. Specify size wanted when ordering. Per dozen pair—any size.......................75c
Note: Single Hoop La Rings in above sizes. Doz....45c
N9386—Hoop La Ring. 8 in. diameter.
Per dozen pair.................................90c
Note: Single Hoop La Rings in 8-inch size. Doz....55c

Add Three Dart Board

B5468—"Add 3" Dart Board Outfit. This board is recommended as the big leader this season. The size of each board is ⅞x16x20 inches. Don't fail to carry a set with you, especially for closed territory. No misses, all sure hits. Add the 3 numbers where the darts have hit and the total represents the number that is used in determining the prize. Full directions accompany each outfit. This is one of the fastest and most interesting games of skill on the market. A full store, 10 or 12 feet frontage, requires 4 boards and 2 dozen darts.
Complete set (4 boards) $8.80

Feather Darts

N9149—Feather Darts. For dart game, turned wood body, weighted, natural finish, one end feathered, sharp steel point on the other. Length 6¼ inches. 1 gross in a box. Doz......................30c   Gro.................$3.00
N9525—Feather Darts. Length 4¾ in., same as above, not weighted. 1 gro. in box. Gro. 90c

Milk Bottles for Milk Bottle Game

Milk Bottles For Milk Bottle Game. Made of well seasoned wood and cast iron

Wood Milk Bottles.
B5151—Pint size. Each. 35c
B5152—Quart size. Each. 75c

Cast Iron Milk Bottles.
B5153—Pint size. Each. $1.25
B5154—Quart size. Each. 2.00

Milk Bottle Sets—Consisting of 6 wood bottles.
B5155—Pint size (6 bottles in set). Set of 6 ....$2.00
B5156—Quart size (6 bottles in set). Set of 6 ....$4.00

Hoop-La-Boxes

Neat, well made basswood boxes with raised bottoms, made especially for Hoop La game. Stained black or brown, with red or green plush lined bottom. Depth ½ inch, furnished in five sizes.

N9387—For 4 inch hoops. Per dozen		$1.15
N9388—For 5 inch hoops. Per dozen		1.20
N9389—For 6 inch hoops. Per dozen		1.30
N9390—For 7 inch hoops. Per dozen		1.40
N9391—For 8 inch hoops. Per dozen		1.60

Novelty Pillow Tops

N9910—Soft leather finish centers, 4 inch sateen borders in assorted bright colors. Beautifully colored designs. The most attractive designs and the biggest flash of color ever shown. We can also furnish a large variety of fraternal and patriotic designs. Specify when ordering, whether art or emblem designs are wanted.
Each .... 40c   Doz............. $4.00

1935 Catalog Page

Novelty Badges

Profitable and popular sellers at all public gatherings. Consists of 50 ligne pin back buttons with snappy and comic sayings and appropriate novelty pendants attached with colored ribbon. Illustrations are about half size.

N9975—Novelty Badge Assortment—One gross, consisting of styles, illustrated on this page. Per assortment (1 gross, no less sold)..$6.00

OH! FIGS LET'S MAKE A DATE
N9961 "Oh! Figs, Let's Make a Date," toy bicycle pendant. Doz. .....45c Gro. $5.00

GO TO IT KID
N9951 "Go To It Kid," toy nipple pendant. Doz. ....45c Gro. $5.00

OH! WHAT A GOOD TIME I HAD LAST NIGHT
N9957 "Oh! What a Good Time I Had Last Night." Doz. ......45c Gro. $5.00

AINT I CUTE
N9973 "Ain't I Cute," celluloid doll pendant. Doz. ......45c Gro. $5.00

DON'T LET NO ONE WOMAN WORRY YOUR MIND
N9970 "Don't Let No One Woman Worry Your Mind." Doz. ......45c Gro. $5.00

WE ARE HIKERS NOT PIKERS
N9963 "We Are Hikers, Not Pikers," two metal shoes. Doz. ......45c Gro. $5.00

I AM NOT MARRIED
N9959 "I Am Not Married," wedding ring pendant. Doz. ......45c Gro. $5.00

GOOD OLD DAYS ALL Forgotten
N9974 "Good Old Days All Forgotten," miniature stein. Doz. ......45c Gro. $5.00

I Love My Wife But No More KIDS
N9968 "I Love My Wife But No More Kids," 2 celluloid dolls. Doz. ......55c Gro. $6.00

THE NATIONAL DRINK
N9971 "The National Drink," metal mug. Doz. ......45c Gro $5.00

IT IS NOT MY FACE BUT MY SHAPE
N9954 "It Is Not My Face But My Shape," doll pendant. Doz. ......65c Gro. $7.50

HELLO BILL
N9958 "Hello Bill!" Toy whistle. Doz. ......55c Gro. $6.00

DON'T MONKEY WITH ME
N9960 "Don't Monkey With Me," toy spider pendant. Doz. ......55c Gro. $6.00

OH! HOW DRY I AM
N9966 "Oh! How Dry I Am," duck pendant. Doz. ......45c Gro. $5.00

SMILE DAM YOU SMILE
N9965 "Smile Dam You Smile," toy mirror pendant. Doz. ......55c Gro. $6.00

GO IT EASY MABEL
N9969 "Go It Easy Mabel," toy nursing bottle pendant. Doz. ......45c Gro. $5.00

I WOULD IF I COULD BUT I CAN'T
N9952 "I Would If I Could But I Can't," large celluloid doll pendant. Doz. ......65c Gro. $7.50

IT'S A LONG TIME BETWEEN DRINKS
N9964 "It's a Long Time Between Drinks," toy watch pendant. Doz. ......65c Gro. $7.50

BEG YOUR PARDON I'M A CHICKEN
N9955 "Beg Your Pardon. I'm a Chicken," large celluloid doll pendant. Doz. ......65c Gro. $7.50

IF YOU FIND THIS CLIMATE TOO COLD GO TO H--L
N9962 "If You Find This Climate Too Cold, Go to H--l," toy thermometer. Doz. ......65c Gro. $7.50

KISS ME DADDY
N9957 "Kiss Me Daddy," large celluloid doll pendant. Doz. ......65c Gro. $7.50

TIE THE BULL OUTSIDE
N9972 "Tie the Bull Outside," toy glass dog pendant. Doz. ......65c Gro. $7.50

SAFETY FIRST
N9956 "Safety First," celluloid doll and safety pin pendant. Doz. ......65c Gro. $7.50

GOT ANYTHING ON TO-NIGHT
N9953 "Got Anything on To-night," toy celluloid doll pendant. Doz. ......65c Gro. $7.50

LEVIN BROS., TERRE HAUTE, IND.

Novelty Badges

Profitable and popular sellers at all public gatherings. Consist of 50 ligne pin back buttons with snappy and comic sayings and appropriate novelty pendants attached with colored ribbon. Illustrations are about half size.

N9999—Novelty Badge Assortment. One gross, consisting of 20 styles, including all designs illustrated on this page except N8555 and N8556. Per assortment (1 gross, no less sold)..............$4.50

N8151   N8152

N8151—"I want to be loved like a baby"—Miniature metal cradle pendant.
Doz..........40c   Gro........$4.50

N8152—"Gee, I wish I had a girl"—Metal aeroplane pendant.
Doz..........40c   Gro......$4.50

N8157   N5158

N8157—"Treat 'em rough" —Miniature metal saw pendant.
Doz..........40c   Gro........$4.50

N8158—"I could Jazz all night"—Miniature band instrument pendant.
Doz..........40c   Gro.......$4.50

N8163   N8164

N8163—"I am Looking for a Sweetheart"—Small metal field glass pendant.
Doz..........40c   Gro.......$4.50

N8164—"Gee, I wish I had a fellow"—Small metal auto pendant.
Doz.....40c   Gro.....$4.50

N8554   N8169

N8554—"When I get you alone to-night"—Miniature metal lantern.
Doz..........45c   Gro........$5.00

N8169—"Oh, Honey give me some"—Miniature band instrument pendant.
Doz.....40c   Gro.......$4.50

N8153   N8154

N8153—"I'm afraid to go home in the dark"—Miniature metal revolver.
Doz..........40c   Gro.....$4.50

N8154—"Everybody's doing it now"—Small metal monkey pendant.
Doz.....40c   Gro.....$4.50

N8159   N8160

N8159—"Won't you be my Teddy Bear"—small metal bear pendant.
Doz..........40c   Gro........$4.50

N8160 — "Matrimonial Prospects"—Small metal key pendant.
Doz.....40c   Gro.....$4.50

N8165   N8166

N8165—"I am the Vampire kid"—Small metal doll pendant.
Doz..........40c   Gro.......$4.50

N8166—"Don't swear, it sounds like Hell" — small metal devil pendant.
Doz.....40c   Gro.......$4.50

N8225—Novelty Badge —50 ligne button with humorous inscription and white metal donkey pendant.
Doz.......45c   Gro... $5.00

N8155   N8156

N8155 — "Member of Knockers Club"—Small metal hammer pendant.
Doz..........40c   Gro.......$4.50

N8156—"Show me where to get a drink"—Small metal camel pendant.
Doz..........40c   Gro.......$4.50

N8161   N8170

N8161—"Let George do it" —Small metal hatchet pendant.
Doz..........40c   Gro......$4.50

N8170—"I am wearing my Heart away for you"—Metal heart shaped pendant.
Doz..........40c   Gro.....$4.50

N8167   N8168

N8167—"Treat me nice or let me be"—Small metal dog pendant.
Doz..........40c   Gro.......$4.50

N8168—"For the love of Mike be reasonable—Miniature metal flat-iron pendant.
Doz..........40c   Gro.......$4.50

N8556—"It ain't gonna rain no mo'"—Miniature white metal camel pendant. Very popular seller at Shriner affairs and all public gatherings.
Doz..........45c   Gro...$5.00

LEVIN BROS., TERRE HAUTE, IND.

Canary Songster, Chenille and Fur Monkeys

Chenille Monkey **Fur Monkeys** **Monkey Jumping Jack**

N8041—Chenille Monkey. Ht. 6 in., composition body and head, chenille covered wire arms and legs in a variety of assorted colors, suspended from good quality wire spring. 1 dozen in box. Doz.....40c Gro....$4.50

N8006—Monkey and Clown Asst.—About 3 in. high, clay figures representing monkeys and clowns, fur covered, string legs with clay feet, spiral spring with ring. Asstd. 1 doz. in box. Doz..........20c Gro..........$2.25

N9563—High Hat Monkey. Ht., 10 in. Flesh-colored composition head, high hat, selected long fur body, heavy brass spring. 1 doz. in box. Doz..........75c Gro......$8.50

N8361 — Novelty Monkey With Voice. Length 7 in., felt covered body, brown with flesh colored face and ears, red cap. 1 doz. in box. Doz. 40c

Bright Colors Always Attract—That's Why We Now Offer This

FINE FUR MONK

in a Variety of Popular Brilliant Shades

NOW You'll Sell More FUR MONKEYS

High Hat Monkey. Metallic cardboard hat, composition head, bright colored fur body, brass wire spring, wood hands and feet. A dandy number for fairs and carnivals. 1 doz. in box.

N4859—Height, 6½ in. Doz.................50c Gro.............$5.00

N8034—Height, 8 in. Doz.................70c Gro............. $8.00

The Jockey Rider Monk Is in the

Forefront of PopularSellers

Concentrate Your Efforts Around This Number and Win More Sales

N8033—Jockey Monkey. Height 9 in., furry figure with composition head, colored flesh, red, white and black, comical expression, with extra long nose, jockey cap, wood hands and feet, cut-out cardboard horse. Suspended on a spiral wire spring. 1 doz. in box.

Gro., $9.50. Special—Doz...... **85c**

YES IT'S THE LATEST
PRESENT BEST SELLER

Brilliant and Attractive in Its Striking Colors

Clown Doll DeLuxe

Be Among the First to Show It

You'll Win Sales and Make Money

N8124—Clown Doll. Length, 13 in.; composition head, colored flesh, red, blue, white and black, red and white polka dot cloth dress, red cardboard arms trimmed with white fur and brass costume bells, green cardboard legs trimmed with fur. 1 doz. in box. Gro...........$9.00 Doz **80c**

Warbles Like a Real Canary

YOU'LL LIKE THIS BIRD

—and what a "whale of a seller"

VICTORY CANARY SONGSTER

Offered at An Amazingly Low Price

N9115 — Victory Canary Songster. Made of metal, finished in canary yellow. The sweet musical notes, trill and warbling of a canary are easily and perfectly produced. The automatic movement of the bill and tail lends a touch of realism Packed one in box.

Gro............$8.50 Doz. **75c**

GELLMAN BROS. MINNEAPOLIS. MINN.

Novelty Wire Spiders, China Dice and
Miniature Figures

No. 2515—Novelty Bisque Dice. New style having countersunk spots in assorted bright colors. Size, 1-inch square. Packed ½ gross in box.
Per gross..................80¢
No. 2526—Novelty China Dice. White glazed finish with assorted color countersunk spots. Size, ¾-inch square. One gross in box.
Per gross..................60¢

No. 2553—Novelty Glass Dice. New style made of dull finished non-transparent glass in assorted bright colors including black, white, orange, blue and brown with contrasting assorted color countersunk spots. Size, ⅝-inch square. One gross assorted colors in a box.
Per gross..................50¢

Large China Dice. Jumbo size slightly round cornered dice made of white glazed china, hollow inside with black countersunk dice spots. Supplied in two sizes.
No. 2529—Size, 1-inch square.
Per dozen..................12¢
Per gross..................$1.25
No. 2530—Size, 1⅜-inch square.
Per dozen..................18¢
Per gross..................$1.75

No. 3081—Miniature Dog Family Novelty. Consists of one large and two small dog figures grouped with basket as illustrated. Made of white bisque with attractive assorted color painted features. A fast selling new novelty! Height, 1¾ inches. Packed one gross in a box.
Per gross..................90¢

No. 2508 — Novelty Bisque Dice. Square design with slightly rounded edges and corners. Unglazed finish with glossy black countersunk spots. A good give-a-way item at an unusually low price. Size, ¾ x ¾-inch square. Packed one gross to the box.
Per gross..................40¢

No. 3079—Miniature Three Monkeys Novelty. Represents the three evils—speak no evil, hear no evil, and see no evil. Attractively made of bisque in brown painted finish with red painted faces and painted eyes. Height, 1⅜ inches. One gross in box.
Per gross..................90¢

No. 3080—Miniature Dog with Cup Novelty. Made of bisque in two-tone black and white colors with contrasting painted features. A new and cleverly designed novelty at an unusually low price. Height, 1⅞ inches. One gross in box.
Per gross..................90¢

No. 2286 — Miniature Shoe and Mouse Novelty. Made of brown painted bisque in the shape of a shoe with silver stripe and gilt finished mouse figure attached in front. An attractive and excellent "give-a-way" novelty at a very low price. Length, 1¾ inches. Packed one gross in box.
Per gross..................85¢

No. 3078—Miniature Birds in Basket Novelty. Made of bisque in assorted bright colors and represents a basket with bird figures on handle and inside, and cat figure on one side as illustrated. A clever new low priced novelty item. Length, 2 inches. One gross in box.
Per gross..................90¢

No. 2142—Novelty Clay Spider. Red painted clay body with yellow decorations and gilt head eyes. The 8 coiled wire legs and feelers tremble when suspended by attached elastic cord with colored celluloid ring at end. Length of body, 2⅝ inches. Packed one dozen in box.
Per dozen..................28¢
Per gross..................$2.95

No. 2113—Novelty Wire Spider. Small size composition body in black color with painted back and spring wire legs and feelers. Legs are in motion when suspended from attached colored string. Length of body, 1½ inches. Packed one gross in box.
Per gross..................80¢

No. 2112—Novelty Wire Spider. Composition body, bead eyes, painted back, 6 coiled wire legs, 2 wire feelers. Each attached to black thread, when suspended, legs are continually in motion. Very realistic. One dozen in box.
Per dozen..................25¢
Per gross..................$2.75

WHOLESALE PREMIUM MERCHANDISE & NOVELTIES

1940 Catalog Page

Novelty Miniature China Animals

A Fine Selection at Attractive Prices

No. 2206—Miniature Dog Assortment. Consists of three assorted dog figures made of highly glazed china with attractive painted features in assorted colors. Average length, 2 inches. Packed one gross assorted in box.
Per gross...................................90¢

No. 2211—Miniature Dog Family. A new novelty set consisting of one large dog and two small dogs made of bisque with realistic painted features. Height of large dog, 1⅝ inches. Put up each set in a wood match box with printed label. Packed one gross sets in carton.
Per gross...................................90¢

No. 5136—Miniature Dogs in Pot Novelty. Cleverly designed of highly glazed white china with realistic painted features and consists of two dogs sitting in a small pot. Width, 1½ inches. Packed one gross in box.
Per gross...................................$1.05

No. 2250—Miniature Sitting Elephant. A novel new ornament made of highly glazed china in assorted lustre pearl effect pastel colors and showing elephant in sitting position. Height, 1 3/16 inches. Packed one gross assorted colors in box.
Per gross...................................50¢

No. 3117—Three Monkeys, representing the three evils, speak no evil, see no evil and hear no evil, made of bisque, painted in natural colors. Height, ⅞ inches; width, 1½ inches. Packed one gross in box. (No less sold.)
Per gross...................................75¢

China Elephant

No. 2207—Miniature Elephant. An appealing and realistic ornament made of highly glazed finish china and supplied in beautiful assorted lustre pearl effect pastel colors. Height, 1⅜ inches; length, 2¼ inches. Packed one gross assorted colors in box.
Per gross...................................$1.15

No. 2256—Miniature Elephant. Realistically made of highly glazed china in attractive assorted lustre pearl effect pastel colors. An unusually appealing ornament. Height, 1 7/16 inches; length, 1 13/16 inches. Packed one gross assorted colors in box.
Per gross...................................65¢

No. 2254—Miniature Dogs in Tub Novelty. A new decorative item made of bisque and consisting of two small dogs with realistic painted features sitting in a small colorfully decorated tub. Length of tub, 2 inches. Put up each set in a wood match box with printed label. Packed one gross sets in carton.
Per gross sets...................................85¢

No. 3064—Novelty Dog Family. Made of highly glazed lustre finish china in attractive assorted colors with painted features and consists of one large dog and two small dogs grouped together. Height, 2¼ inches. Packed one gross in box.
Per gross...................................$1.15

No. 2255—Miniature Dog Assortment. Cleverly designed of highly glazed china and consists of three assorted dog figures with painted features. Average length, 2 inches. Packed one gross assorted in box.
Per gross...................................90¢

No. 3122—Novelty Pin Cushion Assortment. Consists of clever dog figures in assorted positions. Made of highly glazed china with realistic painted features. A small pin cushion is attached to each figure. Average height, 1¾ inches. Packed one gross assorted in box.
Per gross...................................90¢

No. 5135—Miniature Cats in Pot Novelty. Consists of two cats sitting in a small pot. Made of highly glazed white china with painted features. Width, 1½ inches. Packed one gross in box.
Per gross...................................$1.25

No. 2258—Miniature China Animal Assortment. Made of highly glazed lustre finished china in appealing assorted colors and consists of assorted animal figures in clever lifelike poses. Average height, 1½ inches. Packed one gross assorted in box.
Per gross...................................45¢

No. 2282—Boy and Dog Novelty. Consists of a boy doll having small dog figure attached with colored string. Made of bisque with realistic painted features and decorations in bright assorted colors. Height of doll, 2¼ inches. Put up each set in a wood match box with printed cover.
Per gross 95¢

GELLMAN BROS. MINNEAPOLIS, MINN.

LOW PRICED CHINA and BISQUE DOLLS and NOVELTIES

No. 2466—Novelty Charm Assortment. Newest variety of assorted animal, bird and fish figures, made of glass in assorted bright color combinations with colored cords attached to metal rings at top. One gross assorted in box.
Per gross..................................45¢

No. 3130—Miniature Bride and Groom Set. Consists of two miniature china dolls decorated to represent a bride and groom put up in a match box. Height of dolls, 2 inches. Packed one gross sets in box.
Per gross sets..........................90¢

No. 3068—Skull Novelty. Cleverly designed to represent a skull mounted on a book shaped base. Made of bisque in white color with black painted features on skull and colored edge on base. A new and appealing number. Height, 1¾ inches. Packed one gross in box.
Per gross..................................85¢

No. 3164—Miniature Clay Pipes. Assorted shape bowls with reproductions of various animal heads. An excellent novelty that may also be utilized as a cigarette holder. Glazed finish, in assorted bright colors. Packed one gross in box. (No less sold.)
Per gross..................................60¢

No. 3074—Miniature Art Statue Assortment. An excellent new variety of appealingly posed nude figures in three assorted artistic styles. Attractively modeled of bisque in pure white color. Average height, 3⅜ inches. One gross assorted in box.
Per gross..................................95¢

No. 2253—Quintuplets Novelty. An appealing new ornament made of bisque and showing quintuplet doll figures in sitting position with bright assorted color painted features and decorations. Length, 2½ inches. Packed each in a wood match box with printed label, and one gross in carton.
Per gross..................................90¢

No. 2257—Miniature Animal Assortment. Realistically made of bisque and attractively painted in assorted bright colors. Consists of assorted animal figures in a variety of positions. Average length, 1½ inches. Packed one gross assorted in box.
Per gross..................................50¢

No. 3111 — Three Monkeys, representing the three evils, speak no evil, see no evil and hear no evil, made of china, painted in natural colors. Height, 1¼ inches.
Per gross..................................$1.20

No. 2260—Novelty Doll Orchestra Assortment. An appealing variety of boy dolls in assorted positions with various musical instruments. Made of bisque with realistic features and uniforms attractively painted in gilt and assorted bright colors. Average height, 3⅜ inches. Packed one-half gross assorted in box.
Per gross..................................$1.25

No. 2014—Novelty Doll Set. Consists of miniature china doll with moving arms in tin bath tub and put up in a wooden match box having fancy label. Height of doll, 1¾ inches. Packed one gross in box.
Per gross..................................65¢

No. 3067—Skull Novelty. Made of white bisque with black painted high hat and features. A new and extremely realistic low priced novelty. Height, 1¾ inches. Packed one gross in box.
Per gross..................................85¢

No. 3075—Miniature Bird Novelty. Consists of three bird figures mounted on base, and is very attractively made of bisque in assorted bright colors with contrasting painted features. Length, 2 inches. One gross assorted colors in box.
Per gross..................................75¢

WHOLESALE PREMIUM MERCHANDISE & NOVELTIES

GELLMAN BROS. MINNEAPOLIS. MINN.

Fast Selling Decorated Ash Tray
And China Novelties

No. 3126—The newest and fastest selling novelty on the market. Made of china showing a negro boy and bird standing near a fence. Must be seen to be appreciated. Height, 2⅞ inches. Packed one dozen in a box.

Per dozen..................**35¢**
Per gross............**$3.75**

No. 3143—China Out-House Novelty. Painted in bright colors with two colored boy figures. Has a suitable inscription which always brings a laugh. Height, 2¾ inches. Packed one dozen in box.

Per dozen............**30¢**
Per gross......**$3.25**

No. 3119—Out-House Novelty. Made of china and painted in bright colors with two colored boys and inscribed "One Moment Please." A fast selling low priced novelty. Height, 2¾ inches. Two dozen in box. (No less sold.)

Per dozen............**25¢**
Per gross......**$2.75**

No. 5027—Novelty Out-House Ash Tray. Made of brightly painted china with two colored boy figures and out-house at side. Base of tray is inscribed "One Moment Please." Length, 3½ inches. Packed one dozen in box.

Per dozen..................**60¢**
Per gross............**$6.50**

No. 5139—Donkey Barometer and Toothbrush Holder. Decorated figure of donkey made of lustre china with rope tail, and full instructions printed in gilt on brush holder. Length, 3⅝ inches; height, 2½ inches. Packed one dozen in box.

Per dozen..................**35¢**
Per gross............**$4.00**

No. 3125—Novelty China Out-House. Made of orange and green colored china with two black colored boy figures and all other features representing the real thing. Height, 2¼ inches. A laugh provoking novelty and an excellent seller.

Per dozen.....................................**35¢**
Per gross...............................**$4.00**

No. 3129—China Cigarette or Toothpick Holder. Figure of donkey standing on base attached to holder. Highly glazed finish and painted in bright and attractive colors. Length, 3½ inches. Packed one dozen in box.

Per dozen..................**35¢**
Per gross..........**$4.00**

No. 3106—Novelty Out-House Ash Tray. Made of china and consists of oval shaped tray with out-house and two colored boys at end. Brightly painted in assorted colors. Height, 2⅞ inches. Packed one dozen in the box.

Per dozen..................**45¢**
Per gross............**$5.00**

No. 3112—Large Size Novelty Out-House. Made of china and painted in bright colors. An excellent reproduction of an old-fashioned out-house with two negro figures. A fast selling novelty in a new large size. Height, 3⅜ inches. One dozen in box.

Per dozen.....................................**45¢**
Per gross...............................**$5.00**

No. 3127—Imported China Out-House Ash Tray. Consists of a brightly painted oval shaped tray with an orange colored out-house and two colored boys at one end. A new and very amusing novelty. Height, 2½ inches. Packed one dozen in box.

Per dozen..................**55¢**
Per gross............**$6.00**

GELLMAN BROS. MINNEAPOLIS. MINN.

Novelty Honey Bears and Fur Scotties

No. 5515—Extra Large Size "Panda" Bear. Big jumbo size that appeals to young and old. Finely made stuffed body of long pile plush in handsome black and white color combination, with realistic glass eyes and ribbon neck bow, movable head, arms and legs, and when squeezed he produces an attractive voice. A fast seller and an exceptional value at our low price. Height, 27 inches.

Each..............$2.00
Per dozen $23.50

No. 5514 — Extra Large Size Honey Bear. Appealingly made stuffed body of long pile plush in attractive two-tone orange and brown color combination, with realistic glass eyes and ribbon neck bow. Movable head, arms and legs, and when squeezed he produces a pleasing voice. An unusually fast seller at an extremely low price. Height, 27 inches.

Each..............$2.00
Per dozen $23.50

No. 5508—Large Size Plush Bull. A universally popular item. Stuffed body with long pile plush in attractive two-tone black and orange color body. Colored ears with white face, toes and feet. Rolling eyes and daisy flower in mouth. Approximate height, 15 inches; length, 15 inches not including tail.

Each..............$1.15   Per dozen...........$12.75

No. 5506—Large Scotty Dog. Appealingly made of long hair black fur with realistic glass eyes and button nose. When his tail is squeezed, he produces a realistic voice. Supplied with red patent leather effect harness and leash, having nickel plated metal fittings. Unusual sales appeal and quality at an extremely low price. Length of dog, 14½ inches.

Each..................85¢   Per dozen................$9.50

Black and White Panda Bear

No. 5505—Large Size Panda Bear. Popular everywhere, this finely made bear has a stuffed body of long pile plush in striking black and white color combination, with realistic glass eyes and ribbon neck bow. Supplied with movable arms, legs and head. When squeezed he produces an effective voice that pleases all children. A very appealing number at an unusually low price. Height, 24 inches.

Each..............$1.25
Per dozen..............$15.00

Two-Tone Novelty Honey Bear

No. 5504—Large Size Honey Bear. An exceptionally attractive bear made with stuffed body of long pile plush in handsome two-tone orange and brown color combination with glass eyes and ribbon neck bow. Very well constructed with movable arms, legs and head. When his body is squeezed he produces an effective and appealing voice that will appeal to all children. An exceptional value at our low price. Height, 24 inches.

Each..............$1.30
Per dozen..............$15.00

WHOLESALE PREMIUM MERCHANDISE & NOVELTIES

1919 Catalog Page

FELT PENNANTS

NO NOVELTY STOCK IS COMPLETE WITHOUT A LIBERAL SUPPLY OF THESE. STYLES LISTED ON THIS PAGE ARE IN STOCK AND CAN BE SHIPPED IMMEDIATELY

ART PROCESS PENNANTS. ¶ Size 7x18 Per 100 $5.00

We Handle the Most Attractive Styles on the Market.

Our Pennants are made of extra fine felt in assorted bright colors; red green blue yellow purple, etc. Art process letters and designs presenting a very striking effect, put on by a patent process, and will not rub off. Felt strip sewed on wide end, through which cane is placed. Not necessary to tie these, can be put on or taken off in an instant.

We have Pennants worded as follows in stock:

SOUVENIR, SOUVENIR FAIR, OLD HOME WEEK, SOUVENIR CARNIVAL
Any Style, Per 100, $5.00

Note.—We can furnish above pennants with any special inscription desired in lots of 500 without any additional charge. On smaller quantities we make a charge of $1.50 for plate. No extra charge on re-orders. Ten days required on special orders and remittance must accompany order.

AUTO PENNANTS.

N9279. Auto Art Pennants, made of bright colored felt in red, blue, orange and purple, size 12x30 inches. Furnished with the following inscriptions: "Excuse My Dust," "Out for a Good Time," "Safety First," and "Thank You." Any style or assorted. Per 100 ....$10.50

PATRIOTIC PENNANTS.

N9280. Art process pennants, size 12x30 inches, made of blue felt with the inscriptions "The Flag I Love" and "Spirit of 76" with illustration to correspond in bright colors. Either style or assorted. Per 100 ....$10.50

STATE PENNANTS.

N9281. Art Process pennants with name of any state desired and design of Liberty Bell or Flag. Size 12x30 inches, assorted colors blue, red, orange and purple. Five day's time required to fill orders for these. Per 100 (no less sold)..............$10.50

Comic Pennants
12x30
$10.00 per 100

N9282. Reproduction Comic Pennants, made of a good grade of felt in assorted bright colors, size 12x 30 inches. Assorted subjects and appropriate inscriptions. Our stock includes the following:

"Don't Be a Sucker All Your Life."
"Out for a Good Time," "Sept. Morn."
"My Wife's a Suffragette," "Just My Style."
"I Should Worry." "Don't Swear It Sounds Like H—!"

And countless others. The designs are reproduced in bright, flashy colors, and will attract instant attention. No doubt about these selling.
Per 100 ....$10.00

NOTE—Above pennants can be had with any special design desired. Write for prices, stating quantity wanted, and if possible send sketch.

Porcelain Headed Canes,
heads approximately 1¼" to 1¾" diameter.

Porcelain Headed Canes,
heads approximately 1¼" to 1¾" diameter.

Canes, wood and bamboo

1935 Catalog Page

Novelty Canes, Swagger Sticks and Souvenir Whips

Canes, and swagger sticks are profitable sellers at fairs, parks, carnivals. etc. They are in big demand at conventions. celebrations, and for parades.

Swagger Sticks and Parade Canes

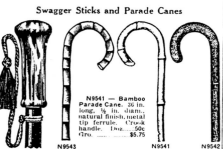

Doll Canes and Sticks

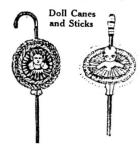

N9541 — Bamboo Parade Cane. 36 in. long, ½ in. diam., natural finish. metal tip ferrule. Crook handle. Doz....50c Gro. $5.75

N9543   N9541   N9542

N8920—Ladies' Swagger Sticks. With wrist cord and silk tassel, large fancy colored wood knob. Bright colored enameled sticks, with nickel tip ferrules. Length, 36 inches. 1 gro. in carton.
Doz. 60c
Gro. $6.75

N9543—Bamboo Parade Cane. 36 in., ¾ in. diam., natural finish. metal tip ferrule, crook handle. Doz.............$1.00 Gro.....$11.50

N9532—Bamboo Parade Cane. 36 in., ⅞ in diam., otherwise same as above. Doz....$1.25 Gro....$13.50

N9542—Parade Cane. 36 in. hardwood in light finish, polished, bent crook handle, metal tip ferrule. Doz.........$1.50 Gro.........$16.50

N9542M—Same as above in mahogany finish, highly lacquered. Doz..........................$2.00

To facilitate shipping and at the same time save you money, we are offering celluloid doll canes and swagger sticks in separate units. Assemble as you want to use them and thereby eliminate breakage in transit.

N9403—Jap Bamboo Canes. Good heavy sticks nicely varnished. Per 100....................85c

N9403X—Same as above, heavier grade, red and green finish. Per 100. ....85c

N8920—Swagger Sticks. Fancy colored knob, wrist loop and metal ferrule. Length. 36 inches. Per gro..........................$6.75

N7011—Celluloid Doll. Length, 4 in. Per 100..2.75

N7000—Celluloid Doll. Length, 5 in. Per 100.. 3.50

N9418—Crepe Paper Dress. Tinsel trimmed, 5½ in. diam. Per 100......................$3.00

Novelty Souvenir Whips at Lowest Prices

Our Souvenir Whips are made of good quality heavy stock and finished in bright colors. Snappers and wrist loops are not included in measurements.

N9538—Whip. 27 inches long, 6½-inch snapper and braided wrist loop. A fancy braided red, white and blue colored web, complete with one molded ferrule. One dozen in package.
Doz. ....35c Gro. **$4.00**

N9539—Whip. 27 inches long, 7-inch snapper and wrist loop. Fancy braided web, shellac finish in assorted bright colors, fancy spiral wound handle with two molded ferrules. One dozen in package. Doz. ....45c Gro. **$5.00**

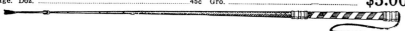

N30—Souvenir Whip, 33 inches long, made of best Java Stock, assorted bright, flashy colors, colored snapper. 6 inch handle. spirally wound with flashy two-color band, white ferrules at each end. Assorted colored strong wrist loops. 1 dozen in a package.
Per dozen ....60c Per gross....................... **$6.50**

N50—Souvenir Whip. Length 36 in. (wrist loop not included in this measure), made from best quality extra heavy Java stock, smooth finish. shellac filled and varnished, asstd. bright flashy colors: yellow, brown, green and sea blue, fancy white ferrules, handles are wound spirally with green, pink, purple and blue celluloid strips, asstd. colored snaps. 4¾ in. wrist loops. 1 doz. in pkg.
Doz. ....65c Gro. **$7.25**

N9099—Lash Whip. Total length 54 in. fancy braided white and black web stock, braided wrist loop with moulded ferrule. 1 dozen in package. Dozen.... ....70c Gross....................... **$7.75**

1935 Catalog Page

LEVIN BROS., TERRE HAUTE, IND.

Carnival Cane Assortments at Lowest Prices

Each assortment contains a large selection of popular, attractive styles, including gilt and silver finish metal heads, with Japanned, ebony and natural finish sticks. All new, bright, clean stock. We guarantee our selections to prove satisfactory. Prices do not include rings or rack. Order separately if wanted.

Carnival Cane Assortments

$3.75 CANE ASSORTMENT.

N9401—Cane Assortment Plain and Japanned sticks Consisting of 85 wood and 15 metal medium sized heads, including styles illustrated above Per assortment (100 canes) $3.75

$4.50 CANE ASSORTMENT.

N9402—Cane Assortment. Consisting of 60 wood and 40 metal head canes. Popular numbers including styles illustrated above. Japanned and natural finish sticks. Per assortment (100 canes) $4.50

$5.50 CANE ASSORTMENT.

N9404—Cane Assortment. Consisting of 60 medium and large size novelty metal and 40 wood heads including the various popular styles illustrated above and many others Per assortment (100 canes)................................$5.50

$6.75 CANE ASSORTMENT.

N9405—Cane Assortment. Consisting of 85 medium and large size novelty metal heads gilt or silver finish and 15 wood heads, including the various popular styles illustrated above and many others. Per assortment (100 canes) $6.75

$7.75 CANE ASSORTMENT.

N9406—Cane Assortment. Consisting of 100 of our largest metal head canes in gilt or silver finish. Natural wood Japanned and ebony sticks. A few styles are illustrated above. Per assortment (100 canes)................................$7.75

Red, White and Blue Canes

N9400—Pine sticks covered with red, white and blue paper in alternate spiral stripes, or in flag paper. Ball tops in colors, canes and heads packed separately to facilitate handling Per 100..............................$ 2.50
Per 1,000...23.50

Cane Racks

Made of extra strong netting, and bound with canvas, well finished and durable brass eyelets in corners, ready to use. Furnished in 3 sizes

N9407	5x5 feet Each	$2.50
N9408	6x6 feet Each	3.25
N9409	7x7 feet Each	3.90

Japanese Souvenir Canes

N9403—Japanese Souvenir Cane. This is the genuine, made by a new patent process. The enamel is baked on and cannot come off. Sticks are all uniform and crook handles, highly enameled and polished mahogany or rosewood color, finely finished. Per 100....75c Per 1,000.. $6.50
N9413—Jap Cane. Same as above, assorted red and green lacquer finish. Per 100.. 85c Per 1,000 ...$7.75

Cane Rack Rings

N9410—1¾ inches in diameter inside measurement, polished natural wood finish, well seasoned. Per 100....$ 1.15
Per 1,000..11.00
N9575—Cane Ring. Same as above, stained mahogany finish. Per 100..$1.50

GELLMAN BROS. MINNEAPOLIS. MINN.

DOLLY CANES, FUR MONKEYS and
CLAY NOVELTIES

No. 3748—Dolly Cane. Alluring 7-inch celluloid doll dressed in bright assorted color feathers with feather decorated celluloid headdress. Complete with bamboo crook canes.
Per 100..................................$5.90
No. 3749—Dolly Cane. Same as above but with 8-inch size dolls.
Per 100..................................$6.95

No. 3718—Dolly Cane. White feather dressed 7-inch celluloid doll with gilt bead earrings. Painted features, jointed arms, metallic paper breast decoration, and assorted silver and gilt wavy hair effect. Complete with bamboo crook canes.
Per 100..................................$5.45

No. 3750—Dolly Cane. Handsome 7 inch celluloid doll dressed in bright assorted color feathers with fancy feather decorated metallic paper hat. Complete with bamboo crook canes.
Per 100..................................$5.90
No. 3751—Dolly Cane. Same as above but with 8-inch size dolls.
Per 100..................................$6.95

No. 2158—Fur Jumping Monkey. Composition head in assorted colors with painted features. Has high-hat in assorted metallic colors and is trimmed with rainbow colored fur. Height, 11 inches.
Per dozen..................................$1.20
Per gross..................................$13.20

No. 2106—Fur Jumping Monkey. Composition head in assorted colors with painted features and metallic colored high-hat. Height, 8½ inches. Two dozen assorted in box. (No less sold.)
Per dozen..................................33¢
Per gross..................................$3.60

No. 2109—Fur Jumping Monkey. Composition head in assorted colors with painted features and metallic colored high-hat. Rainbow colored fur trim. Height, 8 inches. One dozen assorted in box.
Per dozen..................................50¢
Per gross..................................$5.75

No. 2154—Clay Frog. Green body with painted features. Has bright colored fur skirt and spring coil wire arms and legs that tremble when suspended. Elastic cord with wire ring attached at top. Height, 5¼ inches. One dozen in box.
Per dozen 30¢
Per gross $3.40

No. 2117—Clay Devil. Red body with painted features and fur skirt. Has spring coil wire arms, legs, and horns that tremble when suspended. Elastic cord with wire ring attached. Height, 6 inches.
Per dozen..................................33¢
Per gross..................................$3.60

No. 2146—Clay Skeleton. Black body with white trim and spring coil wire legs and arms. Trimmed with colored fur and has metal ring and cord attached. Height, 5¾ inches. One dozen in box.
Per dozen 30¢
Per gross $3.40

WHOLESALE PREMIUM. MERCHANDISE & NOVELTIES

GELLMAN BROS. MINNEAPOLIS, MINN.

Fur Monkey and Feather Dressed Dolly Canes

No. 3718—Rainbow Colored Jumping Monkey Assortment. Monkeys are made with composition heads in assorted colors having painted features and brightly colored metallic high hats. Height, 8 inches. Complete with bamboo crook canes.

Per 100 .... $4.70

No. 3724—Dolly Cane. Newest style 7-inch celluloid dolls dressed in bright assorted color feathers with metallic paper hats in assorted designs and colors. Complete with bamboo crook canes.

Per 100 .... $5.90

No. 3714—Rainbow Colored Jumping Monkey Assortment. Includes an assortment of monkeys made with composition heads in assorted colors with painted features and assorted colored metallic high hats. Height, 6½ inches. Complete with bamboo crook canes.

Per 100 .... $3.15

No. 3712—Dolly Cane. Jointed arm style 5-inch celluloid doll dressed in assorted bright colored feathers with fancy feather head-dress and metallic paper high hat. Striking painted features with gilt bead necklace, assorted silver and gilt painted wavy hair effect, and colored celluloid cane attached to hand. Complete with bamboo crook canes.

Per 100 ....$4.00

No. 3711—Dolly Cane. Attractive 5-inch celluloid doll dressed in bright assorted color feathers with fancy feather decorated metallic paper hat. Jointed arm style with colored celluloid cane in hand. Complete with bamboo crook canes.

Per 100 .... $4.00

No. 3716—Dolly Cane. Jointed arm 5-inch celluloid doll dressed in bright assorted color feathers with fancy feather head-dress and fancy metallic paper hat in assorted styles and colors. Beautiful painted features with metallic paper chest decoration and assorted silver and gilt painted wavy hair effect. Complete with bamboo crook canes.

Per 100 ....$4.00

No. 3733—Novelty Devil Cane. Consists of a realistically designed devil figure made of clay with red colored body, painted features and fur skirt. Has spring coil wire arms, legs and horns and is suspended with elastic cord at top. Trembles continuously when suspended on cane. Height, 6 inches. Complete with bamboo crook canes.

Per 100 $3.40

No. 3732—Novelty Frog Cane. Made of clay with green colored body and brightly colored contrasting painted features. Decorated with colored fur skirt and has spring coil wire arms and legs that tremble realistically when suspended on elastic cord attached to top. Height, 5¼ inches. Complete with bamboo crook canes.

Per 100.. $3.10

No. 3707—Novelty Skeleton Cane. Consists of a realistically designed skeleton figure made of clay with black and white painted body and fur skirt. Suspended with elastic cord and has spring coil wire arms and legs that tremble continuously when hanging on cane. Height, 5¾ inches. Complete with bamboo crook canes.

Per 100 $3.10

WHOLESALE PREMIUM MERCHANDISE & NOVELTIES

GELLMAN BROS. MINNEAPOLIS. MINN.

China Head Cane Assortments, Bamboo
CANES, WALKING CANES AND SWAGGERS

No. 3739—Novelty China Head Cane Assortment. Made with combination black and cherry color fancy striped wood bodies having attractively colored glazed china tops in assorted styles including dice, baseball, dog and elephant designs. Supplied with bright colored fancy silk tassels and nickel finished metal ferrule tips. Length, 35 inches. Packed one dozen assorted in bundle.
Per dozen...............................65¢
Per gross.............................$7.20

No. 3721—Novelty China Head Cane Assortment. Made of enameled wood in assorted bright colors with attractively colored glazed china tops including dice, baseball, dog and elephant designs. Supplied with bright colored fancy silk tassels and nickel finished metal ferrules at tips. Length, 35 inches. Tied one dozen assorted in bundle.
Per dozen...............................60¢
Per gross.............................$6.75

No. 3727—Gent's Walking Cane. Made of wood with heavy mahogany enameled finish and fancy celluloid band near shaped crook handle having assorted fancy foil decorations. Supplied with nickel finish metal ferrule tip. Length, 36 inches. Packed ½ dozen assorted designs to bundle.
Per dozen...............$1.30
Per gross............$14.50

No. 3741—Bamboo Walking Cane. Made of jointed bamboo in natural finish with dark burnt ring trim and shaped crook handle. Supplied with nickel finished metal ferrule tip. Length, 36 inches. Packed one dozen in bundle.
Per Dozen
70¢
Per Gross
$8.00

No. 3715—Bamboo Walking Cane. Jointed flexible bamboo cane finished in natural colors. Crook handle. Metal ferrule. Length, 35 inches.
Per Dozen
40¢
Per Gross
$4.25

No. 3728—Gent's Walking Cane. Heavy black enameled wood with fancy celluloid band near shaped crook handle having assorted fancy metal foil decorations. Supplied with nickel finished metal ferrule tip. Length, 36 inches. Packed ½ dozen assorted designs to bundle.
Per dozen...............$1.30
Per gross............$14.50

No. 3738—Gent's Walking Cane. Made of wood in glossy enameled combination black and yellow striped design with fancy celluloid band near shaped crook handle. Supplied with metal ferrule tip. Length, 36 inches. Packed one dozen in bundle.
Per dozen...............$1.20
Per gross............$13.80

No. 3726—Gent's Walking Cane. Heavily lacquered in combination black and cherry color fancy striped design with correctly shaped crook handle and metal ferrule tip. A popular new design at a remarkably low price. Length, 36 inches. Packed one-half dozen in bundle.
Per dozen...............$1.20
Per gross............$13.80

No. 3746—Gent's Walking Cane. Appealing new style made of wood in combination light and dark brown fancy striped finish with shaped crook handle and nickel finished metal handle band and ferrule tip. Approx. length, 36 inches. Packed one dozen in bundle and one gross in carton.
Per dozen.........................85¢
Per gross....................$9.50

No. 3747—"Chesterfield" Colored Walking Cane. Attractive new style made of wood in assorted red, green, orange, and blue enamel finishes with black enameled shaped crook handles. Supplied with nickel finished metal handle bands and ferrule tips. An exceptionally fast selling cane at an extremely low price. Approximate length, 36 inches. Packed one dozen assorted colors in bundle and one gross in carton.
Per dozen......................70¢
Per gross....................$7.75

No. 3706—Ladies' Swagger Canes, with silk cords and tassels and large size fancy rainbow colored carved heads. Bright colored sticks, with nickel tip ferrules. Length, 36 inches.
Per dozen 50¢
Per gr....$5.75

WHOLESALE PREMIUM MERCHANDISE & NOVELTIES

GELLMAN BROS. MINNEAPOLIS, MINN.

First Quality Toy Whips and Novelty Canes

No. 3734 — Novelty Cane. Made of bright colored felt in the shape of a pair of ladies' pants, with lace trimming and ribbon ties. Printed on both sides with assorted comical sayings as illustrated. Complete with bamboo crook canes.

Per 100 $4.25

No. 3752—Heart Canes. Large size imitation red leatherette heart with stitched edges and red bow at top. Both sides worded "My Heart Belongs to Daddy." Hearts expand to about 1-inch thickness. Size of heart, 9x9½ inches. Complete with bamboo crook canes.
Per 100.................................$4.50

No. 3753—Heart Canes. As above but in gold color with wording "I'm the Guy With the Heart of Gold." Complete with bamboo crook canes.
Per 100.................................$4.50

No. 3735—Novelty Tail Cane. Consists of a ribbon tied bright colored card printed on both sides with assorted comical sayings, and having bushy genuine fur tail attached at bottom as illustrated. Complete with bamboo crook canes.

Per 100 $4.25

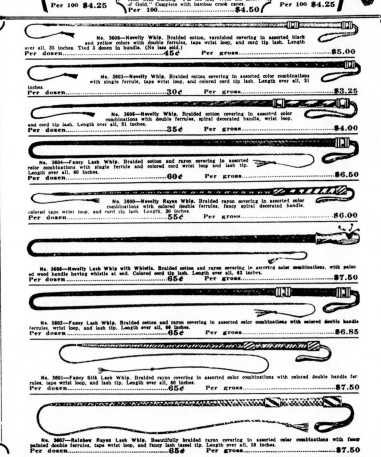

No. 3608—Novelty Whip. Braided cotton, varnished covering in assorted black and yellow colors with double ferrules, tape wrist loop, and cord tip lash. Length over all, 35 inches. Tied 3 dozen in bundle. (No less sold.)
Per dozen.................................45¢   Per gross.................................$5.00

No. 3603—Novelty Whip. Braided cotton covering in assorted color combinations with single ferrule, tape wrist loop, and colored cord tip lash. Length over all, 31 inches.
Per dozen.................................30¢   Per gross.................................$3.25

No. 3606—Novelty Whip. Braided cotton covering in assorted color combinations with double ferrules, spiral decorated handle, wrist loop, and cord tip lash. Length over all, 31 inches.
Per dozen.................................35¢   Per gross.................................$4.00

No. 3604—Fancy Lash Whip. Braided cotton and rayon covering in assorted color combinations with single ferrule and colored cord wrist loop and lash tip. Length over all, 60 inches.
Per dozen.................................60¢   Per gross.................................$6.50

No. 3600—Novelty Rayon Whip. Braided rayon covering in assorted color combinations with colored double ferrules, fancy spiral decorated handle, colored tape wrist loop, and cord tip lash. Length, 30 inches.
Per dozen.................................55¢   Per gross.................................$6.00

No. 3605—Novelty Lash Whip with Whistle. Braided cotton and rayon covering in assorted color combinations, with painted wood handle having whistle at end. Colored cord tip lash. Length over all, 61 inches.
Per dozen.................................65¢   Per gross.................................$7.50

No. 3602—Fancy Lash Whip. Braided cotton and rayon covering in assorted color combinations with colored double handle ferrules, wrist loop, and lash tip. Length over all, 60 inches.
Per dozen.................................65¢   Per gross.................................$6.85

No. 3601—Fancy Silk Lash Whip. Braided rayon covering in assorted color combinations with colored double handle ferrules, tape wrist loop, and lash tip. Length over all, 60 inches.
Per dozen.................................65¢   Per gross.................................$7.50

No. 3607—Rainbow Rayon Lash Whip. Beautifully braided rayon covering in assorted color combinations with fancy painted double ferrules, tape wrist loop, and fancy lash tassel tip. Length over all, 58 inches.
Per dozen.................................65¢   Per gross.................................$7.50

WHOLESALE PREMIUM MERCHANDISE & NOVELTIES

Cane Assortments, Cane Rack Nets, Wood Rings, Etc.

No. 3705 — Patriotic Canes with red, white and blue paper covering and wooden knobs. Length, 35 inches. Put up one hundred canes in bundle, and one hundred knobs in cloth bag.

Per hundred canes, complete

$2.75

No. 3740—Novelty Metal Head Cane Assortment. Popular new variety made with assorted color bamboo bodies and colorfully painted metal heads in assorted styles including parrot, claw, elephant and horse designs. Supplied with nickel finished ferrule tips and colored silk tassels attached at heads. Length 36 inches.

Per 100 canes $5.00

No. 3743—Parade Canes. Made with highly gloss finished paper covering in assorted bright solid colors with round wood knob at end. Length, 35 inches. Put up one hundred canes in bundle and one hundred knobs in bag.

Per hundred canes, complete

$2.75

No. 3650—Wood Cane Rack Rings. Accurately turned of well seasoned hard wood in natural finish, especially for cane rack use. Inside diameter, 1¾ inches.

Per 100...... $1.45

No. 3651—W... Rings. Made of hard wood. Accurately ... turned especially for .... Inside diameter, 1¾ inches.
Per 100.............$1.45

No. 3652 — "Half Dollar" Size Wood Rings. Same as above but smaller size for knife racks, peg games, etc.
Per 100 ....$1.45

CANE RACK NETS

Our cane rack nets are especially made to give long and satisfactory service. Constructed of good quality cord in ¾-inch mesh with sturdy 1½-inch drill binding on edges and brass grommets in each corner. Supplied in four popular sizes.

No.	Size	Price, Each
3700	4x5 feet	$1.75
3701	5x5 feet	$2.10
3703	6x6 feet	$2.80
3704	7x7 feet	$3.50

No. 1007—Pint Size Wood Milk Bottles. Made of well seasoned and accurately turned hard wood in natural finish. Standard pint size for milk bottle game.

Each............................40¢
Per set of six........$2.25

No. 3729—Novelty Head Cane Assortment. Made with assorted colored bamboo bodies, having painted composition heads in assorted styles, including dice, baseball, skull, Scotty dog, comic head and bulldog designs. Supplied with nickel finished metal ferrule tip and colored silk tassel attached at head. Length, 36 inches. One dozen assorted to bundle.

Per dozen........................50¢
Per gross.........................$5.50

No. 1010—Pint Size Aluminum Milk Bottles. Sturdily made of cast aluminum in hollow style with white printed finish. Standard pint size for milk bottle game.

Each........................90¢
Per set of $5.00

EVANS' HIGH STRIKER

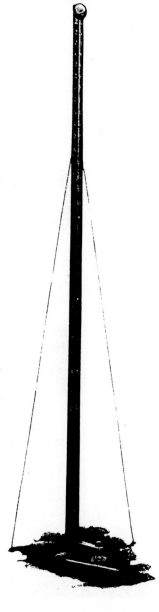

In the Evans' High Striker we offer the Concessionaire a High Striker that is new and different from anything of this kind ever put on the market before. It is made after the plans and specifications of C. H. Allton, who has no doubt had more practical experience with strikers than any other one man in the country. The outfit is strictly high class in every respect, strong and substantial, made of the best materials throughout.

The outfit consists of one 30 foot standard 9 inches wide and 2½ inches thick, mounted on a hardwood plank, 54x12x3 inches thick, and fitted with a 10 inch bronze gong, two mauls, three special steel cables and three of our new improved stakes, together with a monkey wrench and screw driver.

The standard is made of selected hard wood handsomely painted and varnished, numbered from 100 to 3,000. The chaser track is of machine steel, bolted to the standard, making it firm and free from vibration. The chaser is of tool steel, handsomely nickel plated and polished and accurately fitted to the chaser track, making it ride smooth.

The striking beam is 39x6½x3 inches thick with a rubber striking cushion of the best para rubber at one end, the opposite end being fitted with a tool steel spring which transmits the blow from the striking beam to the chaser. The plank base of the striker is reinforced and bound with half inch bolts which extend entirely through the plank from side to side. This prevents warping or splitting and the whole outfit is designed to stand hard usage.

Special attention is called to the three steel cables which we supply with each outfit. These have many times the strength of rope and each cable is fitted with quick connections and turn buckles. Also with each outfit we furnish three of our specially designed metal stakes. These are easily set out and so constructed that they are rigid yet may be removed easily. This is a big saving in time and trouble for the operator as it eliminates the necessity of carrying heavy wood stakes which are unsatisfactory. Weight 230 pounds.

No. 20A68 Complete **$65.00**

No. 20A351 Extra 10 inch gong . . each 8.00

No. 20A349. Extra rubber bumper . . each 5.00

No. 20A348. Extra maul . . . . each 5.00

Notice: We also furnish the above outfit with our special attachment which permits the operator to work strong and to protect himself.

No. 20A352 Complete with special attachment **$100.00**

EVANS' SPECIAL BASE BALL

This Ball is made especially for concessionaires' use and is the most practical ball ever produced for road use. Made of heavy waterproof material carefully sewed in colored thread. Strong and substantial, regulation size.

No. 30A57. Per dozen...........................**$0.60**

WOODEN BALLS FOR ROLL DOWN TABLES AND JAP BOWLING ALLEYS

All these balls are made of kiln dried, thoroughly seasoned maple nicely finished.
No. 30A59. 2 inches in diam...Each **$0.05**
No. 30A60. 2¼ inches in diam......................................Each .06

HOOP LA HOOPS

These Hoops are made of select hardwood finely polished, natural wood finish.
No. 30A202. 3 inches in diam. ....Dozen pairs **$0.50**
No. 30A71. 4 inches in diam.....................................Dozen pairs .40
No. 30A72. 5 inches in diam.....................................Dozen pairs .42
No. 30A73. 6 inches in diam.....................................Dozen pairs .44
No. 30A74. 7 inches in diam.....................................Dozen pairs .46
No. 30A75. 8 inches in diam.....................................Dozen pairs .48

HAND DARTS FOR DART GALLERIES

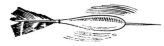

This is a scientifically correct dart, perfectly balanced and weighted with tempered steel point and feather tip. Length 6 inches.
No. 30A78. Per dozen.................... **$1.50**

HUCKLEY BUCK OUTFITS

Huckley Buck is a game that is universally known and always popular. Can be operated with merchandise of any kind and is permitted everywhere as a game of science and skill. The kegs are made of oak 9¼ inches high and 7½ inches in diameter in the center, bound with four iron straps making them very strong. This game is usually framed using ten kegs set in a triangle, but six may be used if preferred.
No. 30A199. Kegs only ....Each **$1.00**
No. 30A57. Baseballs for above.
........................Doz. .60
We also furnish the 3½-inch wooden balls for the old style large kegs.
No. 30A68. .... Each **$0.35**

WOODEN KNIFE RACK RINGS

Our Knife Rack Rings are extra heavy in quality, 1¼-inch inside measurement, finished in mahogany. Rings come 50 to the bundle.

No. 30A70. Per 100 . . . . **$0.85**

DICE BOXES AND MATS

RUBBER DICE MAT

This is one of the best and most practical dice mats on the market. It is made of rubber with raised edge and covered throughout with green billiard cloth, making it absolutely noiseless. Size 17x23 inches.

No. 30A02 ....Each **$3.50**

SQUARE WOOD DICE MAT

This dice mat is of good design, 17x23 inches in size and proof against warping. It is felt lined throughout, with a 1½-inch rim at the back which is tapered down to ⅝-inch on the players' side. This forms a good backstop for the dice without catching or interfering with the player's arm or cuff.

No. 20A13 ....Each **$3.50**

HALF ROUND WOOD DICE MAT

The advantage of this mat lies in the fact that it is made in the form of a semicircle, the straight side with a ⅝-inch rim being the players' side while the half circle has a 1½-inch rim forming a backstop for the dice. This mat is 17x32 inches in size but does not cover the stock in a showcase nearly so much as the ordinary oblong mats.

No. 20A14 ....Each **$3.50**

SOLE LEATHER DICE BOXES

These boxes are made of best quality sole leather, hand sewed, and will last indefinitely.

No. 30A07 Size 3¾x2¾ ....Each **$0.75**

No. 30A10 Size 3½x2¾, velvet finish for shaking first flops.
....Each **1.00**

No. 30A11 Size 3¾x2¾, velvet finish, large size..........Each **1.50**

Our Special for 10 dice. This box is made of selected stock with rim sewed inside the box at the top to trip the dice coming out. This box positively prevents any manipulation of the dice by would-be sharks and is a big protection for all cigar games.

No. 30A09 Size 4x3¼ ....Each **$1.50**

BASE BALL POOL DICE

We are making a special set of Dice for operating Baseball Pools, consisting of three ⅝-inch octagon shaped celluloid dice, numbered from 1 to 8. Each dice is a different color, colors being red, white and blue, representing three different leagues. These dice have proven much more satisfactory than the old style balls and bottle.

No. 10A163 ....Set of three **$6.00**

We are prepared at all times to make special shaped Dice of any size or material. We can furnish 10, 12 or 18 sided Dice, prices on application.

THE SEALED BOOK

Contains an expose of various methods employed by so-called "sharks" covering dice, cards, slot machines and games of every description.

No. 30A205 ....Each **$2.50**

Red and Black Pencils

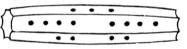

The Evans' Red and Black Pencils are the latest pocket novelty on the market. In appearance they are the same as any ordinary pencil, three sides red and three sides black, however, it is possible in rolling them to cause them to stop on either red or black as desired. Sold two to the set, one controlled and one fair.

No. 20A01. Per set $3.00

High and Low Spinning Tops

A pocket novelty that cannot be surpassed, can be made to come high or low numbers as desired. Simple to operate and can always be depended upon.

No. 30A03. Polished bone. Each $1.50

No. 30A04. Genuine Ivory. Each .. $3.50

Chive or Trick Knife

This is another pocket novelty, one that never grows old. Knife is specially made with two locks, one outside and one secret. Secret lock is simple and well made; nothing to get out of order. A money maker in any spot.

No. 20A06. Each. ...$7.50

Evans' Rolling Logs

Made of selected polished bone to come high or low; red or black; odd or even. A pocket piece that will furnish amusement by the hour. Will pay for itself in ten minutes.

No. 30A05. Each................$2.50

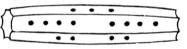

Pocket Roulette Wheels

The pocket Roulette Wheel in the hands of any "live wire" will prove a good investment. Always works, nothing to get out of order and can be made to come high or low at will. Made of aluminum, 3½ inches in diameter, weight 6 ounces.

No. 20A03. Each. $2.50

Chinese Dice Box

Made of polished hard wood, this box is just the right size to carry in the pocket. Shake the dice without removing the cover from the box and name the faces on the dice that are up.

No. 20A02. Dice Box only, each $5.00

No. 10A212. Dice for above, set of three .... .50

Price complete $5.50

Spinning Coins

These are special coins of German silver, made with a head on one side and tail on the other. One coin is made to spin heads, one to spin tails and one fair.

No. 20A05. Set of 3.........$1.50

THE STAR HOOP LA OUTFIT
FOR CANDY, SMALL DOLLS, POODLES, ETC.

This outfit consists of 100 assorted color poker chips, four nickel plated stars, and one dozen 4-inch hoops.

Poker chips are spread out on a table 6x6, and the stars arranged fairly close to the edge. Hoops are sold three for 10c, and prizes distributed according to whether the hoop falls over one of the stars, or over one of the various colored chips. Chips or stars must be completely covered. Stars are used for big prizes, chips for small prizes, which are assorted to correspond with the different color chips.

No. 20A75	Stars for Hoop La Game	Each	$0.50
No. 30A71	4-inch Hoops for Hoop La Game	Dozen	.40
No. 30A188	1½-inch Etched Poker Chips, assorted	Per 100	1.25

(Price, complete, $3.65)

TEDDY BEAR HOOP LA HATS

The Teddy Bear Hoop La Hats have met with great success, one dozen of the hats being used with one dozen Bears. The hats are attached to the bears' heads and the player who succeeds in ringing the hat wins the bear. These hats can also be used with poodle dogs, dolls or other merchandise. Made of metal, handsomely painted and can be used anywhere as a game of skill.
No. 20A72 Hats only....Each $1.25

No. 30A71 4-inch Hoops for above ......Doz. .40

WATCH A LA BLOCKS

In the Evans' Watch a La Blocks we offer the concessionaire the only safe method of using valuable watches on a Hoop La stand. Our blocks are made of hardwood, nicely finished, the watch pocket velvet lined. A few of these blocks on any Hoop La stand will more than double the play and you are perfectly safe in using Elgin movements for prizes.
No. 20A72 Blocks only ....Each $1.00
No. 30A73 6-inch hoops for above. Doz. .44

HOOP LA BOXES

Our Hoop La Boxes are of the very best quality, solid wood block, with an oak moulding handsomely finished. Bottom of the box is lined with velvet, making them very attractive. These boxes are far superior to any other box on the market and will stand any amount of hard usage.

No. 20A74	Boxes only	Doz.	$4.00
No. 30A74	7-inch Hoops for above	Doz.	.46
	Sample boxes	Each	.50

MEXICAN BOWLING ALLEY

The Mexican Bowling Alley stands in a class by itself, as it is the only roll down that it built into a carrying case which can be carried as baggage. For this reason it has met with great favor, especially where playing small attractions and the delay and expense of shipping must be avoided.

The outfit consists of one handsome imitation leather carrying case, which opens at the end. The alley, which has 48 holes, is built in one side of the case, the other side being arranged for the display of prizes and flash. The end of the alley is fitted with a tip-up tray, from which eight marbles are tipped onto the alley, rolling down into the various holes. Each hole is numbered and the player receives the prize bearing the same number as his total score. Size of case 20x36x5, weight complete 18 pounds.

No. 20A59 Complete with marbles..................**$20.00**

SIX-BALL ROLL DOWN TABLE

This is the regulation Roll Down Table, 5½ feet long and 15½ inches wide, fitted with hinged tip-up tray. This outfit is too well known to need any detailed description, may be operated everywhere and never fails to get a play. Table is made of hardwood, finished with two coats of spar varnish, a practical table that will stand any amount of wear and tear.

No. 20A60 Table only ....Each **$9.70**
No. 30A59 2-inch balls, set of 6... .30
Price, complete 10.00

TEETER TAUTER ROLL DOWN

The latest and most popular roll down on the market. Board is 30 inches long, 13 inches wide, handsomely finished and weighs only 7 pounds. One of these games will take the place of two six-foot tables and will grind twice as fast.

With this outfit the operator never touches the balls. The player presses down the high side and the balls roll to the pockets at the opposite end. Six small marbles are used, rolling into twelve numbered pockets. Numbers on the pockets into which the balls roll are added together and the total indicates the prize player receives. Numbers 6, 7, 8, 9, 10, 11, 12, 30, 31, 32, 33, 34, 35 and 36 are large prizes, balance of numbers small prizes.

No. 20A62 Complete with marbles... **$7.50**

THE SUNBURST CANDY PERCENTAGE WHEEL

The Sunburst Candy Percentage wheel is the most handsome and flashy percentage outfit ever produced. The wheel is 56 inches in diameter and the entire face is covered with French plate mirror glass. Around the outer rim of the wheel forty miniature electric lamps are placed, all metal work handsomely nickel plated.

In the center of the wheel a large acorn shaped glass dome is mounted under which four electric lights are placed. When the wheel is revolved these flash on and off alternately, red, white, blue and green, making a most handsome display. The glass in the center section of the wheel is done in ornamental design and the numbers around the wheel are in silver crackel on a red background.

The wheel is intended for a five cent play with candy. When the wheel stops one of the lights in the dome always remains lighted which shows the size of package received by the winner. A red or white light calls for a one pound box, blue a two pound box and green a three pound box. The percentage is correctly arranged and when operated in this manner the operator will net an attractive profit. When it is desired, the operator may use dolls and other high grade merchandise by operating for a ten cent play.

This outfit is made in the same high class manner as our Electric Lighted Paddle Wheel which has always been such a success. It is strong and substantial throughout,, absolutely trouble proof. For list of supplies see Electric Lighted Paddle Wheel.

No. 20A355 Complete as illustrated............................   ....$250.00
No. 20A26   Extra center dome.......................................Each **3.50**
No. 20A28   Extra Mazda lamps for center, any color...................Each **.50**

SUITCASE PERCENTAGE WHEEL OUTFIT

To meet the demand for a high-class percentage wheel we offer the suit case outfit shown herewith, which is the neatest and most practical ever produced.

The wheel is 18 inches in diameter, made of three-ply thoroughly seasoned wood and hand-painted in bright, flashy colors. The pins are nickel plated and bolted through the rim with nut and washer on the back. The wheel is mounted on an attractive nickel-plated post, with ball ornament and fitted with leather indicator with hickory tip. This post is easily taken apart for packing.

The carrying case is 19 inches square, covered with imitation leather, lined throughout and fitted with lock and key.

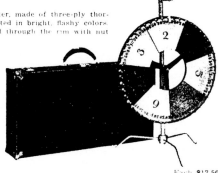

No. 20A124	7 Space Outfit	Each **$17.50**
No. 20A125	8 Space Outfit	Each 18.00
No. 20A120	Imitation leather pads extra	Each 15

RED, WHITE AND BLUE CANDY PERCENTAGE WHEEL

The percentage wheel shown herewith is of special design, particularly adapted for a five-cent play using candy.

The wheel is 23 inches in diameter, built up of thoroughly seasoned wood, three-ply and mounted on an upright pedestal with good bearing. The wheel is attractively painted in contrasting colors, the divisions around the rim being done in red, white and blue, with four red, two white and one blue division to each space on the wheel. The red calls for a half pound box of candy, the white a one-pound and the blue a two-pound.

This is the only wheel with which it is possible to use three different size boxes, which is so important to the successful handling of candy.

No. 20A128	10 Space Wheel and Stand	$10.00
No. 20A129	12 Space Wheel and Stand	11.00
No. 20A120	Imitation leather pads, extra. Each	15

DOLLAR PERCENTAGE WHEEL

Our Dollar Percentage Wheel is 18 inches in diameter mounted on a hardwood post, with a good bearing. This is intended primarily for a money wheel and may be had spaced as shown or with two extra 30's if desired.

The wheel is built up solid of three-ply thoroughly seasoned wood and painted in bright, flashy colors, outfit knocks down for carrying. A thoroughly dependable wheel at a moderate price.

No. 20A115	7 Space Wheel and Stand	$9.00
No. 20A116	8 Space Wheel and Stand	9.50
No. 20A117	Painted tin trays extra	Each .10
No. 20A120	Imitation leather pads extra	Each .15

LITTLE "BIG SIX" TRADE MACHINE

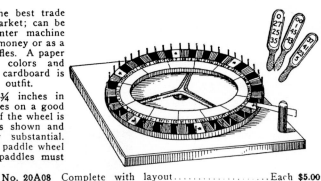

This is one of the best trade machines on the market; can be operated as a counter machine for merchandise or money or as a paddle wheel for raffles. A paper layout printed in colors and mounted on heavy cardboard is furnished with each outfit.

The wheel is 11¾ inches in diameter and revolves on a good bearing. The face of the wheel is divided in colors as shown and the outfit is very substantial. When operated as a paddle wheel a set of 12 wood paddles must be used.

No. 20A08 Complete with layout..................Each **$5.00**
No. 20A43 Wood paddles, extra set of 12................. **1.25**

DIXIE STAR POINTER

This wheel on any cigar counter will pay for itself many times over every day. It is one of the neatest and most compact trade stimulators on the market, being but 7 inches in diameter.

The wheel is made of cast steel, handsomely finished in enamel with gold figures and is operated with a celluloid indicator. This outfit can be used for raffles or as a friendly game for cigars or trade, it is practically indestructible and weighs about two pounds.

No. 20A09 Complete as illustrated ....Each **$1.50**

DEWEY CUBE GAME

This is one of the most fascinating trade games on the market and can also be used for money. The outfit consists of 5 special dice, one cardboard chart or layout and one leather dice box.

The dice are of special design with inlaid faces in colors and the whole outfit is very attractive with a good percent for the operator. The game is intended for a five cent play, rewards payable in merchandise or cash.

No. 10A166 Dewey Cubes, Set of 5 **$2.50**

No. 30A07 Leather dice box....
.... Each .75

No. 10A169 Cardboard layout.....
.... Each .25
Price complete...... **3.50**

THE DEWEY CUBE GAME

PLAYER MUST THROW A PAIR OF HIS COLOR TO WIN

★	STAR PAYS	$1.00 For 5 cents
◉	TARGET PAYS	$1.00 For 5 cents
●	BLUE PAYS	75 cents For 5 cents
●	YELLOW PAYS	50 cents For 5 cents
●	GREEN PAYS	25 cents For 5 cents
●	RED PAYS	10 cents For 5 cents
●	BLACK PAYS	10 cents For 5 cents

N. B. DEALER ALWAYS TAKES AMOUNT PUT UP BY PLAYER WHETHER HE WINS OR LOSES

138 **ATTRACTIVE GAMES**

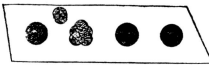

BLACK HAWK FAMILY

This Rack is an attractive Ball-throwing game. For Picnics, Carnivals and Bazaars. The figures are made of 2 inch lumber. Hinged to the frame, reset from counter. Figures are from 10 to 16 inches high and 4 to 5 inches wide. Flashily painted. Frame made from 2x3 lumber. Bolted together. Easily set up. Size 4 feet high, 5 feet wide, complete with canvas background. Price complete **$15.00**

SPOT THE SPOT GAME

A GAME OF SKILL

The most fascinating game ever produced. Will hold a crowd wherever introduced. The object of the game is to cover the spots completely with five plates. This outfit consists of 1 hand painted layout and 20 plates. Price complete **$5.00**

BIMBOO

THE DARKY

Something entirely new in the game of skill which is bound to attract attention and get the play wherever set up. The object of the game is to knock the cigar from Bimboo's mouth and put his eye out by throwing baseballs at him. If the player does this he wins a prize.

The game is made from 2-inch hardwood and will stand the hardest knocks. Beautifully painted in realistic style. Size 4 feet high, 2 feet wide. Reset from counter.

Price Complete **$25.00**

STUFFED PIGS

A new and attractive ball game that will get top play.

Filled with the best wood wool and covered with 10 ounce canvas hand painted in flashy colors, both sides alike. Mounted on solid blocks, 14 in. high. The object of the game is to knock down 3 pigs with 3 balls.

Price Per Set of 3 Pigs........**$6.00**
Price of Balls, Per Dozen.... **1.00**

SLACK MFG. CO.   **CHICAGO, ILL.**

RING AND BALL·GAME

133

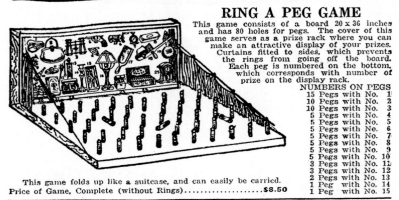

RING A PEG GAME

This game consists of a board 20 x 36 inches and has 80 holes for pegs. The cover of this game serves as a prize rack where you can make an attractive display of your prizes. Curtains fitted to sides, which prevents the rings from going off the board. Each peg is numbered on the bottom, which corresponds with number of prize on the display rack.

NUMBERS ON PEGS

15 Pegs with No. 1
10 Pegs with No. 2
10 Pegs with No. 3
5 Pegs with No. 4
5 Pegs with No. 5
5 Pegs with No. 6
5 Pegs with No. 7
5 Pegs with No. 8
5 Pegs with No. 9
5 Pegs with No. 10
3 Pegs with No. 11
3 Pegs with No. 12
2 Pegs with No. 13
1 Peg with No. 14
1 Peg with No. 15

This game folds up like a suitcase, and can easily be carried.
Price of Game, Complete (without Rings)..................$8.50

MERCHANDISE ASSORTMENT FOR RING A PEG GAME

Consists of 500 pieces—such as a Boudoir Lamp, Pearl Necklace, Watch, Clock, 26-piece Silver Set, Toilet Set, Compact, Necklaces, Bracelets, Fobs, Vest Chains, Cuff Links, etc.
Price of 500 pieces (without game).................................$17.50

We also make up an assortment of 1,000 pieces of high class flashy articles.
Price, Complete (without game)...................................$32.50

NEW COON IN BARREL

Here is something different. Object is to knock figure from top; make him appear at the bung hole. Knock him from the bung hole; make him appear at the top. Works automatic and requires no ropes or cords of any kind. Size 36 inches high. Made of 2 inch lumber.

Price complete $25.00

STUFFED CATS

The cats are extremely popular and a rack made up with them is very appealing and is sure to get the play.
Made of 8-oz. duck thoroughly waterproofed and double seamed, 12 inches high and stuffed with sea grass, mounted on 2 inch maple blocks 4 inches across and 7½ inches wide, with double strength bottom. Painted both sides alike. Price per set of four $5.75

EXTRA HEAVY STUFFED CATS

The cats are made of double 8 oz. canvas, one fitting into the other and stuffed with sea grass. This makes the cats doubly strong and stuffing cannot sag or powder up. Have 2 inch block in base, two with weights and two without. Also has band around bottom to protect them at base. Painted both sides alike, stand 14 inches high.
Price per set of four $9.00

Mason's Chuck Luck Cages

No. D-19

Mason's Miniature Little Neck Cage

SIZE 4 inches high, 2½ inches in diameter, weight 6 ounces. Easily carried in pocket and gives the opportunity to deal under conditions which have been impossible before we offered this small type cage.

Mason's Hand Chuck Luck Cage

SIZE 10½ inches high and 4¾ inches in diameter. Suitable for Chuck Luck or Hazard. Operated with ¾ or ⅝ inch dice.

No. D-21   Mason's Hand Chuck Luck Cage
$10.00

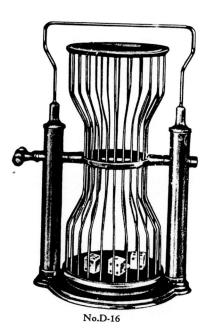

No. D-16

No. D-21

Mason's Standard Little Neck Chuck Luck Cage

WHILE suitable for outdoor use it is generally used for club room play. The cage part is 15½ inches long, and 7½ inches in diameter, 19 inches in height. Attractive appearance. Operated with either ¾ or 1 inch dice. Not furnished with bell unless ordered.

Bingo Equipment, Chuck-Luck Cages

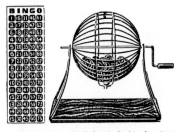

No. 932—Bingo Cage with Equipment. Consists of a strong 9-inch diameter wire globe with hinged door and lead number catch, mounted on a green finished wood base. Supplied with 75 hardwood numbered and lettered balls, ⅞-inch diameter, and one regulation ball chart. Equipped with turning handle having composition grip, and when rotated the lead catch picks up one ball at a time. Can be used for corn game operation. Base size, 7x13½ inches.

Per outfit complete....................$3.50

No. 935—Bingo Cage with Equipment. Popular style consisting of a sturdy 8-inch diameter nickeled wire globe mounted on a handsome maple finished wood base having removable inclined ball chute. Equipped with marble effect composition standards and handle. Delivers one ball at a time automatically as globe is turned. Supplied complete with set of 75 numbered and lettered everlasting black composition balls and one regulation ball chart as illustrated. Made expressly for corn game operation. Base size, 6x12 inches.

Per outfit complete....................$7.50

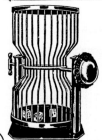

No. 931—Large Size Chuck-Luck Cage. Very well made with heavy metal frame, highly polished and nickel plated. Has large bell which rings when the cage is turned. This is a very popular game and an excellent money maker. Supplied complete with three dice and green felt lay-down having printed numbers. Height, 18 inches. Packed each in box.

Each

$10.50

No. 930—Chuck-Luck Cage. This popular game is now so low in price that every club, church or other similar organizations can own one. Very well made of metal and will give long and satisfactory service. Supplied complete with three dice and green felt lay-down having printed numerals. Height, 11 inches. Packed each in carton.

Each............$2.25

French Miniature Wheels

French Miniature Wheels are complete in every detail, 12 inches high overall, 8 inches in diameter, made very durable, perfectly machined and balanced. Painted very flashily. The rim, made of the finest selected wood, is ¾ inches thick. The hub is of die-cast metal, very ornamental, and will last indefinitely. The workmanship is comparable to our larger wheels, made to scale, and can be used in even more places than the larger wheels. Can be used for merchandise, P. C., or Chuck Luck. Clubs give this wheel especial favor. An excellent amusement item which never fails to get returns!

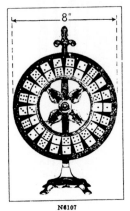

N6107

THE UTMOST IN PORTABILITY AND ADAPTABILITY

$5.50 EACH ANY STYLE

ORDER BY NUMBER

N6101—12 Number Candy Wheel.
N6102—Chuck Luck.
N6103—Club Wheel.
N6104—Baseball Wheel.
N6105—8 Number P. C.
N6106—120 Number Paddle Wheel.
N6107—Pee Wee.
N6108—60 Number Paddle Wheel.

Its very low cost is the least indication of its value. Paper chart furnished with each wheel. Packed one in carton.

Price, complete with stand, any style
Each **$5.50**

Mason's Jumbo Dice Wheel

OUR Jumbo Dice Wheel is the most *practical* and *handsome* one ever produced.

The wheel measures 58 inches in diameter and revolves freely on special ball bearings. It is mounted on a heavy standard 8 ft. high, supported by three heavy metal feet. The standard is topped with a decorative *Chromium silver finish* ornament, which holds the heavy leather clapper.

The dice faces are made of white celluloid, artistically done on a royal blue background covered with clear glass, center sections made of silver crackle glass in ornamental design.

All metal work *Chromium silver finish*, and rim through which the pins are bolted is done in gold bronze.

Mason's Standard Chuck Luck
and Red and Black Wheel

*M*ADE entirely of black walnut, highly finished, makes a wonderful *"flash"*; an extremely popular item due to its handsome and attractive appearance. Can be operated for either Chuck Luck or Red and Black. Both games can be dealt at once and play quickly handled by using our combination layout. Supplied with indicator as illustrated or rubber ball which makes it noiseless. The wheel is 23 inches in diameter revolving on special bearings, and divided into 48 spaces, painted red and black, each space showing 3 dice faces. Mounted on a specially tilted heavy base. The pins are bolted through the wheel. The indicator as shown is the best indestructible kind.

Mason's Red and Black Big Six Wheel

THE Red and Black Big Six Wheel has been used years with success and is one of the most *popular* games on the market. The wheel is 58 inches in diameter and revolves on a special ball bearing, mounted on a pedestal as shown, the complete outfit standing 6½ feet high. The face of the wheel is entirely covered with glass, evenly divided around the outer edge, in colored sections, red, black and star. The center of the wheel is covered with silver crackle glass, in ornamental design, giving a very attractive appearance.

All metal work is *Chromium silver finish.* The outfit is constructed so that it is very easily set up or taken down for shipping, and is strong and substantial, without being too heavy to be practical. The outfit is shipped in a specially constructed shipping case, insuring safe delivery.

Mason's Miniature Chuck Luck
and Red and Black Wheel

T O meet the demand for a smaller Chuck Luck and Red and Black Wheel, we have designed our Miniature Style. It is identically the same as our Standard, except in size; the diameter is 15 inches. Made with stationary indicator only.

Mason's Pari Mutuel Layout

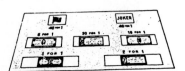

Mason's Pari Mutuel Wheel

OUR Pari-Mutuel Wheel is *rapidly* finding its place in the exclusive resorts. It is easily understood and *enhances* the appearance of the most perfectly appointed rooms. The odds are attractive to the player paying 1, 2, 5, 10, 20, and 40 for 1; however the margin for the house is ample.

The wheel is 58 inches in diameter and revolves on special ball bearings, mounted on an 8 foot pedestal, topped with an attractive ornament. The 48 spaced money combination is arranged with stage money, glass covered. Real money can easily be substituted by the buyer, which adds to the reality and attractiveness of the wheel.

The table is black walnut, 42 x 72 x 36 inches high, beautifully turned and finished, with chestnut top, padded and covered with Simonis No. 1 cloth. Layout is artistically painted in colors on enamel cloth 26 x 42 inches, recessed in top of table and covered with plate glass which is level with table top, allowing a smooth playing surface. All metal parts of wheel and table are Chromium silver finish.

Marble and Jap Roll Down Ball Games

Legitimate, Popular and Profitable.   Games of Skill and Science.   A Prize Given With Each Play.

Jap Roll Down Game

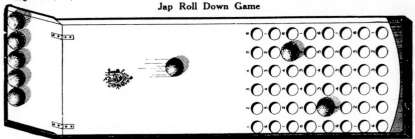

B5488—Jap Roll Down, 4 feet long, 15½ inches wide, made of hardwood in cherry or mahogany finish. Artistically decorated, makes a nice appearance. We furnish 6 wood balls with each board. The principle of the game is to roll the wood balls into the holes all of which are numbered, and add the total. Numbered prizes are displayed on banner and customer is given the article bearing number which corresponds to his total score. Directions for placing numbers (for large prizes, etc.) furnished with each board One person can operate several boards, everybody plays, the young and old alike. Give a prize with every roll and this game can be operated anywhere. Very popular at all parks, fairs, carnivals, picnics, etc. Weight boxed only 20 pounds.
Each complete with 6 balls.. **$6.60**

Complete Prize Assortments For Roll Down Games

B5489—Roll Down Game Assortment of Japanese toys, souvenirs, etc., to be used with the above game, consisting of 30 Capital Prizes, Jewel Cases, Clocks, Dolls, Pillow Covers, etc., 100 pieces assorted Chinaware Vases, Egg Cups, Nut Bowls, Pin Trays, S. and P. Shakers, China Figures, etc. 2,070 Pieces of Japanese give-away premiums, consisting of shell whistles, toys of all kinds, fans, folding mirror books, pictures, pin trays, comic carnival pins, Japanese dolls, bamboo whistles, puzzles, etc. 2,200 pieces in all. Our price for complete assortment... **$30.00**
NOTE—At 5c a roll this assortment brings $110.00. A profit of $80.00.

B5490—Roll Down Game Assortment, same as above but half the quantity. 15 capital prizes, 50 pieces of assorted chinaware and 1,035 assorted give-away items.
Price for complete assortment.. **$15.00**

THE WELL KNOWN AND ORIGINAL
COUNTRY STORE

Disposes of more and greater variety of merchandise than any other similar style or kind of wheel.

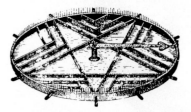

B5497—This is a most unique type of merchandise vender, which not only attracts crowds, but holds them. Perfectly legitimate and allowed to operate anywhere. Pays something every time. Measures 33 inches in diameter, has 30 spaces, 5 for "prizes." Indicator is stationary. "Store" is handsomely painted and revolves on ball bearings, performing quietly and with absolute smoothness. Popular at fairs, bazaars, carnivals, church affairs and other money-raising functions.
Complete. **$11.50**

Revolving Dart Board

This spinning dart board is the game to operate where wheels don't go. Works like a lay-down wheel, with a lay-down chart. Allow one of the players to throw dart at wheel while it is spinning and whoever has money on number in space dart hits wins a capital or intermediate prize. Made of ⅝ in. kiln dried wood, 26 inches diameter, flashily painted. Illustration shows 15 numbers with one red spot to each number. We furnish this board with more or less numbers at the same price.
B5309. Revolving Dart Board.
Each **$6.60**
N9149—Throwing Darts for above game Doz   30c

92

Index

Price Guide

Page 5:   Birds–$15   Dog–$15   Bird Ashtray–$10

Page 6:   Owl–$15   Bull–$15   Collie–$15   Dog with Ball–$15   Pekinese–$12

Page 7:   Staffordshire Dog–$45   Parrot–$35

Page 8:   White Cat–$20   Yellow Cat–$10

Page 9:   Pig–$15   Dog–$15   Elephant 9"x10½"–$15   Elephant 9" x 12"–$25

Page 10:   King Kong–$30 each

Page 11:   Lion–$25   Tiger–$35

Page 12:   All are $15

Page 13:   Snow White–$50   Cowboy–$30   Pinocchio– small $35   large $45

Page 14:   Hula Girl (left)–$25   (middle)–$35   (right)–$25

Page 15:   Hula Girl–$25   Betty Boop–$45   Flapper–$30
Little Egypt–$100 Kewpie Lamp (Arms missing)–$40   (complete)–$80

Page 16:   Kewpie Dolls   (left)–$45   (middle)–$60   (right)–$25

Page 17:   Bag Pipe Girls–$25 each

Page 18:   Drum Majorettes   (left)–$25   (right)–$35

Page 19:   Sweater Girls – $35 each

Page 20:   Mary Had A Little Lamb–$35   Clown–$15

Page 21:   Eagle–$40   MacArthur–$50   Washington (small)–$15   (large)–$30

Page 22:   All are $50 each

Page 23:   Uncle Sam (left)–$35   (right)–$45

Page 24:   All are $50 each

Page 25:   Top - Indian & Sailor–$10 each   Bottom - Indian & Cowboy–$30 each

Page 26:   Feather Girl Cane–$25 Figural Cane–$20 Prop–$400   Cloth Cat–$75

Page 27:   Ornate Roulette Wheel–$1400   Cast Iron Roulette Wheel–$600
Astrological Reading Machine–$800

Page 28:   All are $10 each

Page 29:   Charlie McCarthy   (small)–$30   (large)–$50

Page 30:   All are $35 each

Page 31:   Lone Ranger–$50   Superman–$70

Page 32:   Rooster–$25   Ducks–$45

Page 33:   Dogs at top–$15 each   Elephant (4½")–$10   (9½")–$15
Elephant (right)–$25

Page 34:   Bull Dog–$15   Police Dog–$15   Rin Tin Tin–$45   Pekinese–$50

Page 35:   Oriental Girl–$35 Bathing Girl–$35   Beach Belle–$45   Frenchy–$45

Page 36:   Cat–$30   Lilly Doll–$20   Tootle–$65

Page 37:   Colt & Horse–$20   Jr. Cowboy–$25 Broncho Buster–$60   Buckaroo–$65

Page 38:   All are $10 each

Page 39:   Sheba–$45   Vamp–$60   Ruby–$60   Jumbo–$25

Daisy–$60   Baby–$15

Page 40: All are $15 each

Page 41: Dancing–$35   Fan Dancer–$45   Miss Katy–$50   Rebecca–$60

Page 42: Popeye–$50   Wimpy–$50   Jumbo–$35   Elephant–$25

Page 43: Sport Girl–$25   Horse–$20   Ranger–$65   Indian–$25   Windmill–$20
Ranger on Horse–$25   Bull–$10   Police Dog–$25

Page 44: Gnome–$40   Snookie–$30   Miss Wonderland–$50   Talkie Dan–$50
Bear–$25   Washington–$35   Confucius–$25   Dogs are–$15 each

Page 45: Sailor–$50   Elephant–$25   Carriage–$35   Broncho Buster–$60
Sailor Maid–$25   Charlie McCarthy–$25   All others are–$10

Page 46: Puppet–$45   Ship–$15   Cricket–$45   Bull #685–$15   Elephant–$25
Sitting Bull–$35   Twin Scotty–$20   Scotty–$15

Page 47: Evans' Kutie Kids #40A400–$60   #40A402–$75+
Character Dolls #40A1034–$75+ #40A1002–$75+ #40A799–$100+

Page 48: #468–$40   #469–$75   #470A–$60   #987–$45   #988–$60

Page 49: All are $25 each

Page 50: Cat & Rooster–$35   Medallion–$100   Glass Charms–$15   Eagle–$60
Watermelon Boy–$75

Page 51: All are $10   except Glass Ball Scopes–$50

Page 52: All are $10   except Black Memorabilia–$30

Page 53: Twin Beds–$30 Turnover Ashtray–$15 Hotcha Girl–$15   Squirt Ashtrays–$20

Page 54: #C6248–$100+   #C6247–$75+   #N9305–$2   Milk Bottles $6 ea.,
(wood) $50 set, (cast iron) $75   Hoop-La-Box–$20-30   Pillow–$20
Darts–$5

Page 55: All are $7 each

Page 56: All are $7 each

Page 57: #N8041–$3   #N8006–$2   #N9563–$10   #N8361–$3
Fine Fur Monkey–$10   #N8033–$10   #N8124–$15   #N9115–$2

Page 58: All are $1-2 each

Page 59: All are $1-2 each

Page 60: #2466–$5   #3074–$10   #2260–$5   #3130–$15   #2253–$40
#2014–$20   #3068–$15   #2257–$10   #3067–$25   #3164–5
#3111–$5   #3075–$5

Page 61: All are $30   Except #5130 & #3129–$10

Page 62: #5515–$50   #5514–$50   #5508–$50   #5504–$35   #5505–$50+
#5594–$50+

Page 63: Pennants – All are $20 each

Page 64: All are $20 each

Page 65: All are $20 each

Page 66: All are $10 each

Page 67: Canes are $10 each   Whips are $5 each

Page 68: Figural Canes–$20   Plain Canes–$15   Cane Racks–$10   Rings–$1
Souvenir Canes–$2   Red, White, and Blue Cane–$10

Page 69: Dolly Canes–$20 each   Monkey Canes–$10 each

Page 70: All are $20 each

Page 71: Figural Canes–$20   All others are $5

Page 72: All are $5 each

Page 73: Patriotic Canes–$5 each   Figural Canes–$20 each   Wood rings–$2 ea.
Milk Bottles–$50-75 a set   Cane Racks–$10 each

Page 74: Evans' High Striker–$1000+

Page 75: Baseball–$5   Hoop-La-Hoops–$3-4   Kegs–$30-40   Wood balls–$4
Knife Rack Rings–$2

Page 76: #30A02–$15-20   #20A13–$15-20   #20A14–$25-30   Leather Dice Box–$10-15
Baseball Pool Dice–$25

Page 77: Pencil–$5   Trick Knife–$20   Tops #30A03–$20   #30A04–$50   Rolling
Logs–$10   Roulette Wheel–$15   Chinese Dice–$35   Spinning Coins–$15

Page 78: Star Hoop-La–$1   Teddy Bear–$2   Boxes–$5   Hoops–$2

Page 79: Mexican Bowling–$150   Six-Ball Roll–$250+   Teeter Tauter – $100+

Page 80: Sunburst Wheel–$2500

Page 81: Percentage Wheel–All $225+   Red,White, Blue Percent. Wheel–$400+
Dollar Percent. Wheel–$150+

Page 82: Big Six Trade Machine–$150   Dixie Star–$200   Dewey Cube–$25

Page 83: Black Hawk Family–$400   Spot Game–$20   Bimboo–$250   Pigs–$75

Page 84: Ring A Peg Game–$200   Coon–$300   Cats–$75   Heavy Cats –$100

Page 85: #D-19–$35+   #D-21–$25   #D-16–$150

Page 86: Cages #932–$40-50   #935–$50-60   #931–$150+   #935–$50+
French Wheels–$150

Page 87: $2500

Page 88: $1000

Page 89: $2500

Page 90: Wheel – $500   Layout–$35

Page 91: $2500

Page 92: Jap Roll Down Game–$250+   Country Store–$150
Darts–$2   Board–$100